fascinating
canada

fascinating canada

a book of questions and answers

John Robert Colombo

DUNDURN

TORONTO

Editor: Matt Baker
Design: Jesse Hooper
Printer: Webcom

Library and Archives Canada Cataloguing in Publication

Colombo, John Robert, 1936-
    Fascinating Canada : a book of questions and answers / John
Robert Colombo.

Issued also in electronic formats.
ISBN 978-1-55488-923-5

    1. Canada--Miscellanea. I. Title.

FC61.C644 2011   971   C2011-901172-7

1   2   3   4   5   15   14   13   12   11

We acknowledge the support of the **Canada Council for the Arts** and the **Ontario Arts Council** for our publishing program. We also acknowledge the financial support of the **Government of Canada** through the **Canada Book Fund** and **Livres Canada Books**, and the **Government of Ontario** through the **Ontario Book Publishing Tax Credit** and the **Ontario Media Development Corporation**.

Care has been taken to trace the ownership of copyright material used in this book. The author and the publisher welcome any information enabling them to rectify any references or credits in subsequent editions.
                                                                      J. Kirk Howard, President

Printed and bound in Canada.
www.dundurn.com

Dundurn Press	Gazelle Book Services Limited	Dundurn Press
3 Church Street, Suite 500	White Cross Mills	2250 Military Road
Toronto, Ontario, Canada	High Town, Lancaster, England	Tonawanda, NY
M5E 1M2	LA1 4XS	U.S.A. 14150

Contents

Preface

The Dominion of Canada is a remarkable country in many ways, but some of these ways are contradictory — and that is what makes the country so fascinating. It is seen as a young country, yet it is one of the world's oldest functioning democracies. It is seen to be spacious, yet its landscape is sparsely populated. It is seen to be a country that is neither capitalist nor socialist, for it has a "mixed" economy and many of its most binding social institutions reflect a combination of private initiative and public undertaking — the so-called "crown" corporations. It is seen to be a multicultural country (it pioneered the use of that term to describe a policy that is falling into disfavour), while it retains two official languages and promotes no official culture. It is seen to be a democracy, yet it is a monarchy with not one but two constitutions. It is seen to be a peaceful country (we were the first proponents of international peacekeeping and have adopted a police force as a national symbol), yet we have fought valiantly in most major military engagements. It is seen to be a haven in a heartless world, and indeed more than one-third of its population is foreign-born and most everyone here boasts of his or her ethnic roots. It is seen to be a country with a cold climate, yet the weather differs little from that enjoyed by the citizens of other northern nations. Similarly, it is seen to be a Northern nation, yet most of its inhabitants live as far south as possible. So Canada is a fascinating country indeed!

That is Canada in the abstract, the skeleton of the country that informs the present book. But the present work isn't about Canada as an abstraction — it is instead about the country and its people in their multitude of particulars. The country is a collection of initiatives and interests, many of them quite fascinating for their wisdom and their folly. About seventy years ago, newspaperman Bruce Hutchison described the spirit of this country and its people in a memorable book titled *The Unknown Country: Canada and Her People*. Today, we might argue with the pronoun *her* in the book's subtitle, because we aren't inclined to classify countries by gender, but the adjective *unknown* remains the operative word. Many of us seem to have lost touch with our innate curiosity, especially with regard to this great country, and that is unfortunate, because curiosity is a great and essential gift. Curiosity is a trait that encourages us to wonder about ourselves and other selves, about the sciences and the arts, and ultimately about man's fate and human destiny. In some cultural traditions, this driving force is known as *holy curiosity*, and indeed I hold curiosity to be holy, or at least very special, for it confers the power to enliven and enlighten everyday attitudes, interests, and concerns

For a long time, I have been especially curious about subjects of specific Canadian interest — what is known as Canadiana. I find it fascinating. For the last half-century, I have devoted an hour or so of each day to researching subjects like the ones discussed in this book, and I do so by bombarding myself and friends and the specialists I meet with a barrage of questions, so many questions that at times I must seem to be a know-nothing! Not long ago I met a friend from my university years who upon graduation took a postgraduate degree at Johns Hopkins University and then settled in a suburb of Washington, D.C. He has enjoyed a notable career, initially as director of the Congressional Budget Office, later as an associate of the American Enterprise Institute, and currently as senior fellow with the Urban Institute. I innocently asked him if he had an explanation for the fact that he had been so successful in life, since even he had admitted surprise at the trajectory of his professional career. He pondered this question for a while and then replied, "Yes, I have an explanation."

"What is it?" I inquired.

"I ask questions," he said, innocently. I waited. Then, following a dramatic pause, he added, with a twinkle in his eye, "I ask *dumb* questions."

We both laughed, but then we began to discuss the implications of the word *dumb*. Why would an intelligent, professional person want to ask a dumb, stupid, or silly question? Certainly not to elicit dumb, stupid, or silly answers.

Perhaps the act of asking a peculiar or a provocative question, one that would not immediately occur to a bright person, is a good way to test, to challenge, to brainstorm, to suggest that there are other ways of thinking and acting, ways that are different and more effective than the old ways. A seemingly senseless or insensitive question often leads to a thoughtful and suggestive response. My friend, a political economist by training, found that questioning the basic assumptions and the accepted procedures was a way to probe strengths and weaknesses. Forming the question is a way of framing the answer. In effect, my friend was agreeing with the late Marshall McLuhan, who used to quip, "Ask me a question. Learn something."

In my books I have tried to make available, to the general reading public, important or interesting facts and fictions about the lore, history, and culture of this land and its people. While there are nationalistic and patriotic reasons for this activity, what has motivated me is the need to encourage self-knowledge and, with it, national knowledge. I have always felt that if we learn more about the spaces we inhabit, as well as our national past and our possible future, in the process we will acquire knowledge about ourselves ... as human beings — what we are, what we were, and what we may be.

At the same time, I enjoy positioning our regional knowledge in a national setting and our national setting in a global context. Patriots, jingoists, and boosters like to boast about superlatives: Canada has "the first of this," "the biggest of that," or "the best of everything." In this book there are such points of distinction, to be sure, because I am not immune to their appeal. But I try to back away from simply making or repeating such claims, for such boasting is self-defeating and a form of bullying. As well, one's superlatives are always being called into question or in time are surpassed by other peoples' superlatives. A good instance of this is Toronto's CN Tower, which was "the world's tallest, free-standing structure" from 1976 to 2010, when it was finally eclipsed by the Burj Dubai, now known as the Burj Khalifa, which stands even higher.

Increasingly, I prefer to dwell on subjects of quality, distinction, and ongoing interest. I believe that this approach to national knowledge was in the back of the mind of editor-and-commentator Andrew Coyne when he was interviewed about national goals by the Frontier Centre for Public Policy on March 14, 2007:

> It seems to me our goal should be to make ourselves the highest exemplar of universal values. If we think that freedom is a good thing for the people of the world, let's try to be the freest country. If we think that fairness is a universal human value, let's try to be the fairest country. Let's try to be the most democratic country. That won't necessarily make us different from other countries in terms of the values that we pursue, but I hope that maybe we'll do a better job at it. It means we share in a common heritage to which most of democratic countries subscribe. The goal of trying to be the best rather than trying to be unique is a better and more appropriate objective of national policy.

The command rings true: "Do a better job of it." Coyne finds a national purpose in determining what qualities of life are important and then realizing them nationally and internationally.

My approach to deciding what subjects to include in these pages is based on what excites me and on what I believe may excite the readers of this book, fellow Canadians all. I have a taste for the offbeat, and I find when I indulge it, I attract the attention of other people.

Perhaps the best instance of a feature entry is an offbeat one and a personal favourite. It asks the following question: "Have Canadians contributed to Shakespeare's Globe Theatre in London?" If the wary reader assumes the answer is "yes," the reader is right, otherwise why would the question be asked in the first place? The original Globe Theatre was built on the south bank of the Thames River in London, England, in 1613; the present-day one, a re-creation of the original, was built in 1997. Here is how my research began: My attention was caught by an advertisement in *The Times Literary Supplement* for the Globe's production of *Henry IV*. It featured an attractively designed coat of arms, arms that appeared too modern to be those of King

Henry. This proved to be so when I checked the monarch's armourial bearings on Google, for his appeared to be ancient, whereas the one in the *TLS* looked modern. Then I checked the website of Shakespeare's Globe Theatre and found that the repertory company had commissioned a series of beautifully designed crests, by a noted English designer, for the season's productions. Note that so far there was no Canadian connection at all, though later there would be.

In my research I learned about the history of the Globe and the rebuilding of a facsimile of the original stage on the site of the old one on the Thames, now close to the Tate Modern gallery. In the process I kept coming upon the name of Sam Wanamaker, the American actor and producer who led the restoration project, as well as the name of his right-hand man, theatre historian John Orrell. The latter's name was new to me, so I checked it out. Here, I hit pay dirt! Although born in England, Orrell acquired a doctorate in drama from the University of Toronto and then devoted his academic career to teaching theatre at the University of Alberta. He spent the summers in England, where he researched the skyline of Elizabethan London and advised Wanamaker on the form and structure of the original playhouse. Today, there are plaques on the wall of the reconstructed playhouse to honour both men for their invaluable contributions.

Then I learned about two literature professors in the Maritimes who donated their private libraries of Elizabethan publications to the English company, which named their collection "The Canadian Library." Finally, I discovered the existence, in Toronto, of the Shakespeare Globe Centre of Canada, supporters of the London playhouse. So, Canadians played an important role in the phoenix-like rebirth of the Globe. I asked myself a follow-up question: As Canadians, do we have any connection with the *original* playhouse, where Shakespeare's plays were premiered some four centuries ago? It may have been a *dumb* question, but it yielded a smart answer.

The Stratford Shakespeare Festival is North America's largest classical repertory theatre. It was established in 1953 in Stratford, Ontario, and Tyrone Guthrie, the Anglo-Irish director, a student of the Elizabethan stage, agreed to serve as its artistic director on one condition: he insisted on introducing the so-called thrust stage, known to Shakespeare and his fellow actors, to the modern world. He was able to do so and thereby set the stage for the innumerable new and renewed playhouses that have appeared over the last sixty years. Through my research I was able to show the synergy of ideas that link the original Globe, the reconstructed Globe, and the Stratford Festival Theatre in Ontario. I wrote up my findings and had them vetted by the specialists in London. All of this may sound a bit odd, but it is an instance of serendipity (being interested in an off-beat subject with no obvious Canadian content) as well as an example of associative thinking (linking Globe I and Globe II with Ontario's Stratford). It took more than a month to make these connections, a few minutes here, a few minutes there. The entry that I wrote, greatly condensed, may be read in the present book in the section devoted to ideas. Check the index for its location.

To know parts of ourselves we need to know parts of our country. The reverse is also true, for there is little self-knowledge without national knowledge. Over a hundred years ago, an editor in Toronto wrote, "Canada only needs to be known in order to be great." I believe that this statement applies to the country as a whole but especially to the people who live here. So it is also true that "*Canadians* only need to be known in order to be great." I hope that this book contributes in a limited way to offer its readers that necessary national knowledge and to encourage that essential self-knowledge.

The present book consists of 357 short questions and the same number of long answers. They are loosely arranged, not really in any particular order. I resisted the tendency to group the entries by subject or topic, though from time to time they benefit from this treatment. The book is designed for browsing and for making accidental and serendipitous discoveries. Having said that, let me add that the contents will prove to be useful to specialist readers, because the book does have an the overall arrangement of questions and answers in four general sections: People, Places, Things, and Ideas.

The book's Index consists of more than 500 entries. These references will be of use to the reader, the browser, the researcher, and the specialist in search of names, places, concepts, phrases, etc. Not every reference in the text could be indexed. One caveat: the numbers in the Index are entry numbers, not page numbers.

Acknowledgements

The text of this book was researched and written over many years, so it would be impossible to list the names of all the people and the institutions consulted. But I will recall the names of some men and women who have made signal contributions along the way. Work was conducted at the Metropolitan Toronto Reference Library where the late Mary Alice Neal worked for many years as my research assistant. Specific queries were well handled by my friend, the reference librarian, Philip S. Singer. Also helpful were fellow researchers Dwight Whalen, W. Ritchie Benedict, Edward Butts, as were Cyril Greenland, David A. Gotlib, Mel Hurtig, Tony Hawke, and Bill Andersen. Editors who worked on similar books of mine over the decades have left their mark: Mel Hurtig, Denise Schon, John Pearce, Tony Hawke, Kirk Howard, and Beth Bruder. Dundurn's editors also deserve to be thanked: Matt Baker and Jennifer McKnight. My principal acknowledgement is to my wife Ruth, who fact-checks me all the time!

I'd like to dedicate this volume to my grandchildren: Alex, Julia, James, Findley, and Nicolas. May Canada prove to be a place of continued fascination for you and future generations.

people

001. Are there honorary Canadian citizens?

The Canadian Parliament designated, between 1985 and 2009, six non-Canadians as honorary Canadian Citizens.

Raoul Wallenberg, Swedish diplomat, was accorded this honour in recognition of his efforts on behalf of Jewish people in Nazi-occupied Europe. The award was made posthumously in 1985. Nelson Mandela, former president of the Union of South Africa, received this honour in person in a ceremony in Hull in 2001 to acknowledge his anti-Apartheid leadership. Paul Erickson, Major League baseball player, was named an honorary Canadian in 2001 for his philanthropy and outstanding contributions to Canadian life. Tenzin Gyatso, the 14th Dalai Lama and recipient of the 1989 Nobel Peace Prize, was awarded honorary citizenship in 2006. Aung San Suu Kyi, prime-minister-elect of Burma and recipient of the 1991 Nobel Peace Prize, was awarded this status in 2007. His Highness the Aga Khan, 49th imam of the Shia Ismaili Muslims, became an Honorary Citizen in 2009.

002. Why does the name of a Canadian girl appear in a Harry Potter book?

J.K. Rowling's book *Harry Potter and the Goblet of Fire* is a popular work of fiction that appeared in 2000. In July 1999, while completing it in Edinburgh, Scotland, she received a letter about Natalie McDonald, a nine-year-old Toronto girl who was dying of leukemia and found much comfort in the Harry Potter books. The letter was written by a family friend named Annie Kidder, who requested that Rowling correspond with Natalie by email. Rowling agreed, but her email arrived one day after Natalie's death on August 3, 1999.

Natalie's mother, family, and friend Annie Kidder all began to correspond with Rowling, and a transatlantic friendship developed. Unknown to Natalie's family and friends, Rowling commemorated the young fan, who did not live long enough to read a copy of *Harry Potter and the Goblet of Fire*, by giving the name Natalie McDonald (on page 159 of the first edition) to a first-year student of Hogwarts School of Witchcraft and Wizardry. This sad-but-inspiring story was told by Brian Bethune in the article "The Rowling Connection," in *Maclean's*, November 6, 2000.

003. Did Al Capone go into hiding in Moose Jaw?

Moose Jaw, Saskatchewan, may seem an unlikely place for Al Capone to go into hiding, but the Chicago gangster did disappear for three months in 1926, when U.S. prosecutors wanted to indict him for the murder of fellow gangster Joe Howard. No one knows where Al Capone found sanctuary, but local stories are rife with indications that he took refuge in Moose Jaw.

The city, located on the CPR line with the Soo Line running to Chicago, was easily accessible to Capone. From the early 1920s to the early 1930s, prohibitionists put a damper on the sale of liquor, but gangsters expedited its illegal traffic and trade. It is said that secret tunnels beneath the city's streets were used in the transport of bootleg beverages.

According to reporter Craig Wong, in "Canadian Mysteries: Rumours Rife, Hard Evidence Scant on Gangster Al Capone's Time in Moose Jaw," *The Ottawa Citizen*, July 11, 2001, local traditions boast of Capone's presence in the city whenever there was "heat" in the Cicero district of Chicago, where he established his crime empire.

004. Has Elmer Fudd ever appeared in a cartoon as a Mountie?

Elmer Fudd, the fuddy-duddy cartoon character, played a Mountie in *Fresh Hare* (1942) directed by Friz Freleng, with story by Michael Maltese, animation by Manuel Perez, and musical direction by Carl W. Stalling. He fumbled his investigations with much muttering and stammering. According to film exhibitor Reg Hartt, "This is a great little film but the ending is cut from current prints as it features Black folks."

005. Who was the Le Page of LePage's Glue?

Generations of Canadian and American schoolchildren grew up with small, bell-shaped bottles of glue, or mucilage, as it was called. Each bottle was surmounted by a tip of red rubber. The bottles were labeled, LePage's Glue. The company that manufactured these bottles was founded by William Nelson Le Page (1849–1919), an inventor and businessman who was born on Prince Edward Island, worked in Massachusetts, and died in Vancouver, B.C.

He was a youngster when the Le Page family moved to the United States. He was raised in Massachusetts, where trained as a chemist. In 1876, he established the Russian Cement Company in Gloucester, Massachusetts, which sometime later was renamed the LePage Company. His first glues were formed from fish skins. The company's first product was the "original" glue and mucilage, and bottles of these made "LePage's" a household name throughout North America. Between 1880 and 1887, LePage's sold fifty million bottles of glue worldwide. Today, the company has special expertise in prepared industrial adhesives with long shelf life. It produces a range of adhesive products and is the world's largest producer of private-label, pressure-sensitive tape. Its newest product is Power Grab.

Vanessa Le Page, the great-great-granddaughter of the founder, is a resident of Toronto who collects LePage memorabilia. By 2001, the company's 125th anniversary, she had over 3,000 items in her collection. The items document LePage's history and the wide range of products it produced.

006. Who is the singer Eilleen Twain?

Eilleen Twain is the name given at birth to the popular singer and performer — otherwise known as Shania Twain — by her parents, in her native city of Timmins, Ontario. On the advice of her producer and husband Mutt Lange, she changed the Eilleen part of her name to Shania. This occurred sometime after the year 1988, and success as a composing, performing, and recording artist followed suit. Shania is said to be a woman's name in the Algonkian language of the Ojibway. (The singer's adoptive stepfather is Ojibway.) Nicholas Jennings, writing in "Overture," *Maclean's*, December 3, 2001, identifies Twain as "the highest-selling female artist in the history of country music."

007. Did Mary Pickford ever appear in a Canadian movie?

Mary Pickford (1892–1979), the silent film star who enjoyed so much popularity with audiences in the silent-film period that she was dubbed America's Sweetheart, appeared in 147 short films released between 1909 and 1913 and in fifty-four feature films released between 1913 and 1933, when she retired. A filmography appears in Eileen Whitfield's appreciative biographical study titled *Pickford: The Woman Who Made Hollywood* (1997).

All of these shorts and features were produced in the United States. She never appeared in a Canadian-made movie. Yet of special interest to Canadians is the fact that she was born in Toronto and made special arrangements with the Department of Citizenship to regain her Canadian citizenship before she died.

In one of her movies (and possibly in another), she plays the part of a Canadian woman — an Eskimo lass in *Little Pal* (Famous Players, 1915). Set in the Yukon, the feature film was based on a short story by Marshall (Mickey) Neilan and was directed by James Kirkwood. Pickford played an Inuit girl in a "dispirited style," according to one reviewer. It was greeted with dismay, her biographer Eileen Whitfield noted, perhaps because she hid her well-loved golden curls beneath a long black wig.

One of the short films might have Canadian content and might be set in Nova Scotia. It is called *An Acadian Maid* (Bioscope, 1910). No print of that film is known to survive. No description of its setting or action is known.

So the short answer to the question posed above is "No." She never appeared in a Canadian movie. But she played a role identified with Canada. She has since then been described as "cinema's first superstar."

008. Did Buckminster Fuller have any Canadian associations?

Yes, the American designer and futurist Buckminster Fuller (1895–1983), who is identified with the words "Spaceship Earth," has a number of associations with Canada.

Fuller is internationally known as the creator of the geodesic dome, and the largest and most imaginative of his geodesic domes was the one he designed to house the U.S. Pavilion at Expo 67 in Montreal. It focused attention on American design and technology, and the image of the glass-ribbed dome became an icon associated with this most successful of world expositions.

In his memoirs Fuller mentioned that as a youngster he worked in the machine plant in Sherbrooke, Quebec, where he learned valuable lessons about assembly line production, with its efficiencies and the rationalization of effort.

As an innovative designer, twice he turned his attention to the city of Toronto, which he described in interviews as a city that "works." In the 1960s he prepared "Project Toronto," a three-month-long study of the city and how it works. He recommended, among other imaginative schemes, a floating city for the waterfront, a bold forerunner of the pale Harbourfront complex. In 1972 he promoted "Project Spadina," a vast, futuristic highway that was to fill the ditch remaining from the city's abandoned plans to extend the Spadina Expressway. His projects were utopian, attention-getting, and caused much comment but no commitment.

009. What is the meaning of *Anishinaubaek*?

Anishinaubae is singular for "human being" and *Anishinaubaek* is plural for "human beings." The words may also mean "good human being" and "good human beings." It is the way the Native people known as the Ojibway or the Chippewas refer to themselves in their own language.

010. What are the five basic functions of humanity according to the Ojibway?

Native elder Basil Johnston, writing in *The Manitous: The Spiritual World of the Ojibway* (1995), explains that there are five basic functions of humankind: leading, defending, providing, healing, and teaching. Each function is represented by its "totem," or symbol of a bird, animal, small creature, or fish that served also as a family herald. Johnston explains, "The word comes from *dodaem*, meaning action, heart, and nourishment."

011. What was Immanuel Velikovsky's Canadian connection?

Immanuel Velikovsky (1895–1979) was the principal, modern-day proponent of the theory of catastrophism — the notion that major changes on the Earth's surface are the result of global cataclysms. Scientists recognize that cosmic catastrophes have occurred in the distant past, but they dismiss the theory that they have taken place during the historical period by noting that the geological and cultural records do not support the theory of catastrophism.

Velikovsky was a Russian-born physician and psychoanalyst who studied these records in Palestine, in France, and in his later years in Princeton, New Jersey. He came to public attention with a highly readable book, titled *Worlds in Collision* (1950). It was followed by such best-sellers as *Ages in Chaos* (1952) and *Earth in Upheaval* (1955), in which he marshalled what evidence he could find — geological and cultural as well as psychological — to support his notion that mankind suffered from "cultural amnesia" when "the sky fell down." This perspective allowed him to offer an original account of such mysteries as the parting of the Red Sea, the collision of parts of the planet Jupiter with Earth, the origin of Oedipus, the birth of Christianity and Islam, etc.

The Canadian Broadcasting Corporation was among the earliest of public organizations to take an interest in his theories and to subject them to critical analysis in various radio and television programs, including some in *CBC Ideas*, produced by Robert Zend in the early 1970s. The CBC programs examined the reactions of scientists to such claims.

Velikovsky received an honorary doctorate from the University of Lethbridge, Alberta, which on May 9 and 10, 1974, sponsored an academic conference on his findings and influence. "Velikovsky and Cultural Amnesia" was a multi-disciplinary endeavour with the conference organizers, representing such disparate disciplines as physics, biology, English, and psychology. Its organizer was the physicist Earl R. Milton, who edited the proceedings published as *Recollections of a Fallen Sky: Velikovsky and Cultural Amnesia* (Lethbridge: Unileth Press, 1978). The guest of honour delivered an address with the arresting title, "Cultural Amnesia: The Submergence of Terrifying Events in the Racial Memory and Their Later Emergence."

So it might be said that Canadians "led the way" not so much in espousing Velikovsky's theory of catastrophism as in exposing it to public and academic scrutiny. As the astronomer and writer Carl Sagan noted, scientists are impressed with Velikovsky's cultural evidence, whereas humanists are impressed with his scientific evidence. (Sagan went on to dismiss the latter.) Some of Velikovsky's predictions about planetary atmospheres have been proven true; others, false. His dramatically written books retain a measure of their popularity to this day.

012. Who is "Mussolini of Montreal"?

There have been many bossy mayors of Montreal, including Camillien Houde, but the title "Mussolini of Montreal" belongs to Italy's wartime dictator Benito Mussolini. A full-length, uniformed portrait of him aside a brown horse appears in the fresco painted high above the altar of the Church of the Madonna della Difesa. Il Duce is up there with the angels, cardinals, altar boys, prophets, and carabinieri.

This parish church was the first Roman Catholic church to be built in the Little Italy area of Montreal in 1919, at the expense of the city's Italian immigrant community. The fresco was painted by Guido Nincheri, an Italian-born church artist. It commemorates "the signing of the Lateran Pact of 1929, the agreement between Mussolini and the

Vatican that created the Vatican City State," according to Ingrid Peritz, in "The Mussolini of Montreal," the *Globe and Mail*, August 27, 2002. At the time, Mussolini was a hero in the eyes of the Catholic church. During the Second World War, Nincheri was interned for three months as a fascist sympathizer at Camp Petawawa, Ontario.

The image on the fresco became a national news story during a $4 million restoration program aimed at obtaining recognition for the church as a national historic site. There is no thought of expunging it.

013. What are Babe Ruth's Canadian connections?

The American baseball star hit his first home run in a minor league game at Toronto's Hanlan's Point Stadium, September 5, 1914. Legend has it the ball disappeared into Lake Ontario, an incident described in Jerry Amernic's novel *Gift of the Bambino* (2002).

Baseball historian William Humber, writing in "The Canada Connection," *Maclean's*, September 2, 2002, says, "Ruth's life is a veritable treasure house of Canadiana." He was taught to play baseball by an Xaverian Brother named Matthias, born in Lingan, Nova Scotia. His first wife was Helen Woodford from Halifax, and a Quebec City-born Red Sox owner brought him to Boston. His longest home run was 600 feet at Montreal's Guybourg Ground in an exhibition game in 1926.

Humber has many more tidbits in his column. But these are enough to prove him right when he wrote, "The Sultan of Swat had a lot of the Canuck of Clout in him."

014. Who designed the World Cup of Hockey trophy?

The World Cup of Hockey trophy, so named in 1996, is the victory cup awarded to the winning team in a series of invitational international hockey tournaments. Intermittently scheduled, the World Cup of Hockey replaced the Canada Cup for hockey supremacy, which was first awarded in 1966. The original cup was a bronze affair with a spiky appearance. It consisted of the right half of an upright maple leaf.

The World Cup of Hockey trophy, its replacement, was specially fabricated from a composite alloy of copper and nickel, as well as solid cast urethane plastic. It was designed in 2004 by Frank Gehry, the postmodern architect. He was long a fan of the game and played it in his youth in downtown Toronto near the Art Gallery of Ontario, which he redesigned in November 2008.

015. Was Pierre Elliott Trudeau a serious contender for the position of secretary general of the United Nations?

No. Pierre Elliott Trudeau was a man of numerous achievements and notable accomplishments, but he was never a serious contender for the position of secretary general of the United Nations. The fact that an intensely private, left-leaning law professor was able to attain the office of prime minister of Canada and hold on (with one hiatus) from 1968 to 1984, the year he opted to resign from public life, is perhaps accomplishment enough.

Trudeau's final year in office was played out on the international stage in terms of his well-meaning but hastily conceived world peace initiative. To many observers it appeared that Trudeau was less interested in advocating his peculiar peace plan than he was in promoting himself as a candidate for the highest office of the United Nation — secretary general. How seriously Trudeau sought this office is an open question, but it is generally admitted by U.N. observers that Trudeau was not a serious contender for the position, being distrusted by both the communists and the capitalists. He was also regarded as something of a loose cannon and a social gadfly by the representatives of the unaligned countries. Kurt Waldheim was succeeded as secretary general by Javier Perez de Cuellar of Peru. It is likely, one would imagine, that Trudeau would have had greater impact on the world stage as secretary general than did the lack-lustre Perez de Cueller.

016. What did Lester B. Pearson not say was his greatest disappointment?

Many honours came the way of Lester B. Pearson, including becoming prime minister of Canada between 1963 and 1968. It is an open secret that Pearson, the career diplomat, wanted to be elected to the highest office of the United Nations — secretary general — not to the prime ministership of Canada.

He was a serious candidate for that office on two occasions. In 1946 he was defeated by Trygve Lie of Norway, and in 1953 by Dag Hammarskjold of Sweden. Pearson's sympathies were too pro-American for the Soviets, who much preferred neutralist Scandinavians. Yet, between 1952 and 1956, Pearson served with distinction as president of the United Nations General Assembly, being awarded the Nobel Prize for Peace for his efforts in defusing the Suez Crisis.

It was something of an anti-climax for him to contest the leadership of the Liberal Party of Canada, to endure the taunts of Prime Minister and then opposition leader John Diefenbaker, and for him to head Canada during its centennial year. Canada was not the United Nations; Canadian affairs were not world affairs.

017. Who wrote the score for the musical *Duddy Kravitz*?

Mordecai Richler's novel *The Apprenticeship of Duddy Kravitz* was the basis of both a successful feature film and an unsuccessful musical comedy. The music for *Duddy* was written by Galt McDermot, co-creator of the fabulously successful Broadway musical *Hair*. By all reports, McDermot, who was born in Montreal, composed a lively score for *Duddy*. The production opened at the Citadel Theatre in Edmonton, where it bombed. It reopened at the National Arts Centre in Ottawa, in May 1984, where it bombed again. It has not been heard from since, but given the prominence of the author and the composer, it is not likely to lie fallow forever.

018. Who took the photograph that appears on the cover of Rush's 1984 album?

The rock band Rush posed for the camera of famous portrait photographer Yousuf Karsh of Ottawa, and the image was reproduced for the cover of their 1984 album *Rush*.

019. What success story was told in the CBC-TV movie *Breaking All the Rules*?

Breaking All the Rules, which premiered on CBC-TV in 1987, told the story of the invention and marketing of the Trivial Pursuit board game. The game's originators are two Canadians: John Haney and Scott Abbott. The game was conceived in 1981 at the Jester Arms Inn at Stratford, Ontario After a rocky year and a half, the concept caught on, and before long everyone, it seemed, was playing Trivial Pursuit.

020. Which painter did Oscar Wilde praise as "the Canadian Constable"?

The Anglo-Irish writer Oscar Wilde toured Central and Eastern Canada in 1882. At an exhibit of art in Toronto in May, he saw a painting called *Fleeting Shadows*. The pastoral landscape of Waterloo County impressed him as a work with "soul" and "feeling." Wilde felt the artist to be "an exceedingly clever fellow" and proclaimed him "the Canadian Constable." In an address later that evening at the Grand Opera House, Wilde praised the painting for being "full of the highest art and beauty."

Fleeting Shadows was painted by a young artist named Homer Watson (1855–1936), who was a native of Doon, Ontario, and a self-taught artist with no social connections. His career was given a great assist by Wilde, who commissioned a landscape painting of his own and helped secure additional commissions from friends in the United States. When the painter made his first trip to England in 1888, Wilde introduced Watson to Whistler with these words: "Mr. Watson is the Canadian Constable, and Barbizon without ever having seen Barbizon." These details are noted by Kevin O'Brien in *Oscar Wilde in Canada: An Apostle for the Arts* (1982).

021. Who was the only French Canadian ever to meet Victor Hugo?

Today, it is difficult to imagine the degree to which Victor Hugo (1802–1885) dominated the cultural life of France and French-speakers throughout the world in the second half of the nineteenth century. The only English writer to be compared with the great literary Frenchman is Charles Dickens. Yet, the English novelist was less versatile than the French *littérateur*. Hugo, after all, was not only a novelist, but also a leading poet and dramatist — and Dickens lived only fifty-eight years to Hugo's eighty-three.

Victor Hugo's life and work mightily impressed Louis-Honoré Fréchette (1839–1908). The Quebec poet and *littérateur* was accorded recognition as the unofficial poet laureate of French Canada and was the first Canadian to be honoured by the illustrious Academie Française. Fréchette initiated a correspondence with the Hugo. In an address delivered before the Royal Society of Canada in 1890, Fréchette recalled how ten years earlier he had been received by the great French writer, then in resident of the isle of Guernsey. Fréchette greeted Hugo as one "saluted by the entire universe." Hugo replied that Fréchette was a victim of "the follies of Louis XV" during whose reign France lost Quebec.

It was Fréchette's suggestion that he was probably the sole French Canadian ever to meet Hugo — or at least to be received by him.

022. Which American president is remembered in Quebec as *le petit juge*?

The American president William Howard Taft (1857–1930) served from 1909 to 1913 as the twenty-seventh president of the United States.

Thereafter, he served as chief of the U.S. Supreme Court from 1921 until his death. Taft had an association with French Canada that is recalled to this day. For the last thirty-eight years of his life, Taft summered at the family lodge at Murray Bay, the resort community on the north shore of the St. Lawrence, known today as La Malbaie. The French Canadians were fond of *le petit juge* — the little judge — for Taft was short of stature but outgoing and friendly in nature. In fact, it is Taft who as president established the "special relationship" that was said to have existed between Canada and the United States until the Trudeau administration in 1968.

023. Was Benjamin Franklin's son a traitor?

Benjamin Franklin's son is judged a traitor to the cause of American independence, but not to the British and Canadian cause of the Imperial connection.

Benjamin Franklin was one of the signers of the U.S. Declaration of Independence. His son, William Franklin, served as governor of New Jersey. Identified with the British during the Revolutionary War, he was arrested as a spy, jailed for two years, and deported to England. In England he enjoyed the perquisites of a lifetime pension.

Interestingly, William's son, William Temple Franklin, was an American patriot and stuck with his grandfather.

024. What is Canadian about "The One Who Got Away"?

The One Who Got Away is the title of a British movie released in 1957. It was directed by Roy Baker and shot in Switzerland, despite the fact that the setting was Canada. It told the true story of Franz von Werra, a German pilot (played by Harvey Kruger) who had the distinction of being the sole prisoner of the Second World War to escape from a Canadian internment camp. He succeeded in making his way to the still-neutral United States, where he generated publicity for the Axis cause.

025. Who is the father of anthropology?

Many anthropologists consider Joseph-François Lafitau to be the father of anthropology. He has also been called the father of ethnology, anthropology's cousin discipline. A Jesuit from France, Lafitau served as a missionary among the Mohawks at Caughnawaga. From 1712 to 1729, he observed the life and customs of the Natives and described them in *Jesuit Relations*. He identified the ginseng plant growing in the St. Lawrence valley and was thus responsible for the profitable trade in the plant, which continues to this day. One of his notions, since discredited, was that because the Iroquois had many customs in common with the Lycians — who lived in what is now southwest Turkey — the Natives of North America are their descendants.

026. Was Glenn Gould a fictional character?

Glenn Gould, the celebrated pianist, died in Toronto in 1980. As a recording artist, he has reached an immense audience of classical music lovers. As a fictional character, he has made appearances in two works of fiction. He figures in Austrian author Thomas Bernhard's novel *The Loser* (1991) and in American author Richard Powers's *The Gold Bug Variations* (1991). In both novels he is described as a hermit-like performing genius alienated from his country and century. Robert Fulford discusses these novels in this column in *Saturday Night*, September 1992.

027. Who were "Your Eminent Residences" at the Stratford Festival?

Tyrone Guthrie, artistic director of the Stratford Festival, was wryly amused when he arrived in Stratford to find in his company a house, a hut, and a mews — the talented actors Eric House, William Hutt, and Peter Mews — so he addressed them as "Your Eminent Residences."

028. Who rode Scout?

Tonto, the faithful Indian companion of the Lone Ranger, rode a pie-bald Indian horse known as Scout. The Mohawk actor Jay Silverheels, a Native of the Six Nations Reserve near Brantford, Ontario, played Tonto on radio, television, and in the movies in the 1940s and 1950s. The Lone Ranger rode "the great horse Silver."

029. Who composed the women's anthem "Give Us Back the Night"?

The words and music of the women's anthem "Give Us Back the Night" were composed by Cynthia Kerr, the Hamilton songwriter; the French translation was prepared by Chantal Chamberland.

The anthem's chorus runs as follows: "Who's going to break this silence, who's going to fight the fight? / Stand up and be counted, and give us back the night. / Who's going to break this silence, who's going to fight the fight? / Stand up and be counted, and give us back the night." When the chorus is repeated the third time, the following words are added: "Give women back the night."

Kerr composed and copyrighted the moving anthem on October 17, 1989, as if in anticipation of the Montreal Massacre of fourteen women students at l'Ecole Polytechnique in Montreal, December 6, 1989. The anthem is now performed at the annual vigils that commemorate the massacre. An audio cassette, *Give Us Back the Night / Redonnez-Nous la Nuit* (Open Mind, 1989), includes the following notice: "We dedicate this recording to the fourteen women whose dreams were crushed on December 6, 1989, at l'Ecole Polytechnique, Montréal." The cassette lists the names of the background vocalists, all of whom are Hamilton-area students. One of the vocalists was Nina de Villiers, who was slain the night of August 9, 1991.

030. Did A.H. Clough compose any verses in Canada?

This is a trick question. Arthur Hugh Clough, the Victorian versifier, did not visit any part of Canada on his trip to America. But he crossed the Atlantic in the summer of 1850 aboard the steamer *Canada*, and in his berth he wrote the lines of one of his moving poems, the one that begins like this: "Green fields of England! wheresoe'er / Across this watery waste we fare, / Your image on our hearts we bear, / Green fields of England, everywhere." The incident is described by David Williams in *Too Quick Despairer: A Life of Arthur Hugh Clough* (1969).

031. Who is the Ottawa-born comic writer and actor whose name is most frequently misspelled?

That question sounds like a comedy routine from the typewriter of Dan Aykroyd, the Ottawa-born comic writer and actor who got his start with SCTV's Second City stage troupe and TV's *Saturday Night Live*, later moving on to such feature films as *Ghostbusters* and *Spies Like Us*. His name is frequently misspelled by the media and on movie marquees.

032. Who was the second premier of Newfoundland?

Everyone knows that J.R. (Joey) Smallwood was the first premier of Newfoundland. He held office from 1949 to his resignation in 1972. His successor was Frank D. Moores, who held office from 1972 to 1979.

033. Did someone named Robur ever go over Niagara Falls?

This happened only in the pages of Jules Verne's *Master of the World* (1904). In the 1914 English-language version of this fantastic adventure novel, Robur the Conqueror is a master criminal who nurtures an insane ambition to rule the world. As captain of the *Terror* — a combination automobile, boat, submarine, and airplane — he flees two pursuing destroyers on the Niagara River and then sweeps over Niagara Falls and sails away. Verne wrote, "At the moment when the *Terror* reached the very edge of the Falls, she arose into space, escaping from the thundering cataract in the centre of the lunar bow."

034. Who created Superman?

Superman, the first of the caped crusaders, was created in 1939 by writer Jerry Siegel (1914–1996) and cartoonist Joe Shuster (1914–1992). They met in Cleveland, where Jerry lived. Joe was a youngster from Toronto, and the *Daily Planet*, where Lois Lane and Clark Kent worked, is modelled on the *Toronto Daily Star*, which he had delivered house to house. It is frequently said that Americans claim Superman whereas Canadians claim Clark Kent.

035. What were John Buchan's favourite Canadian books on angling?

John Buchan, Lord Tweedsmuir, served as governor general of Canada. Born in Scotland, his country home lay in the Border region. He was a confirmed angler and a discerning *littérateur*. He could tell a good book from a mediocre one, especially when it came to angling. Here is what he wrote about the conjunction of literature and fishing in *Memory Hold-the-Door* (1940):

The literary classics of angling after all are few in number, for who is there besides [Izaak] Walton? I should select part of the *Noctes Ambrosianae*, and some of Andrew Lang's *Angling Sketches*, but that may be a Borderer's bias; Lord Grey of Fallodon's *Fly-fishing* beyond doubt; and two Canadian books, Stewart Edward White's *The Forest* and W.H. Blake's *Brown Waters*. But Walton must always head the list.

It is interesting to note that histories of Canada writing and writers yield no information on Stewart Edward White. W.H. Blake's well-written *Brown Waters* was published in 1915; its sequel is *A Fisherman's Creed* (1923).

036. What was the so-called Champagne Safari?

What has been called the Champagne Safari was the 1,200-mile expedition across the Canadian Rockies in the 1930s led by Charles Bedaux. The millionaire industrialist travelled in style with a fleet of Citroens, 130 horses, and gourmet food and books. He was accompanied by his wife, his mistress, and the cinematographer Floyd Crosby, who kept a record of the "trek." In 1995, director George Ungar worked the footage into the film *The Champagne Safari*. The Canadian experience was the highpoint in Bedaux's life — he was a Nazi sympathizer who was arrested for treason, eventually committing suicide in 1944.

037. Did Joachim von Ribbentrop ever visit Canada?

Joachim von Ribbentrop was a German aristocrat, royalist, and careerist who, swallowing principle, befriended Adolf Hitler and joined the Nazi Party. He ashamedly offered it the benefit of his contacts, experiences, and talents. He spent 1910 to 1914 in Canada, except for a short visit to Germany and a stint as a journalist in New York City. Von Ribbentrop learned to speak British English as a young man, and the British Empire impressed him as a system of government and trade. In subsequent years he tried to convince Hitler of the need to mingle some aristocrats among the ambitious non-aristocratic officers and to restore the Hohenzollern monarchy to Germany and Austria. The details appear in John Weitz's biography *Hitler's Diplomat: The Life and Times of Joachim von Ribbentrop* (1992).

038. Who lives in the residences known as Rideau Cottage and 11 Rideau Gate?

Rideau Cottage and 11 Rideau Gate are two residences located on the grounds of the estate known as Government House or Rideau Hall, the official residence of the governor general.

Rideau Cottage was erected by the first governor general, Lord Monk, and it subsequently served as the residence of the governor general's secretary.

A temporary residence for official guests who for one reason or another have not been offered rooms in Rideau Hall itself, 11 Rideau Gate has no permanent residents.

039. Was Terry Fox the subject of a song written and sung by Rod Stewart?

Rod Stewart, the American hard-rock singer and performer, headed a benefit in Boston, Massachusetts, on August 5, 1989, to honour the memory of Terry Fox — the marathon runner who died at the age of twenty-two in 1981. Stewart wrote and performed a song titled "Never Give Up on a Dream." It includes such lines as "Inspiring all to never lose, / It'll take a long, long time for someone to fill your shoes. / It'll take somebody who is a lot like you, / Who never gave up on a dream." Its royalties are earmarked for cancer research.

040. Who was the last Canadian combatant killed during the Second World War?

The last Canadian combatant killed during the Second World War was Lieutenant Robert Hampton Gray, a Royal Canadian Navy Volunteer Reserve pilot and a native of Nelson, B.C. He was posthumously awarded the Victoria Cross for bravery. He was twenty-seven years old when he died.

Gray was killed early in the morning of August 9, 1945, the day an atomic bomb was exploded over Nagasaki. Flying a Corsair launched from the desk of a British aircraft carrier, he was able to sink an enemy warship, but was caught in enemy fire. With his Corsair crippled, he crashed into Onagawa Bay. A memorial to his bravery was erected on August 9, 1989, at Sakiyami Park, which overlooks Onagawa Bay on the Honshu coast of Japan. The memorial was the first on Japanese soil to honour a foreign serviceman.

041. Are there years that Canadian athletes have failed to win gold medals at the Olympic Games?

Canadian athletes are among the world's best, despite government programs that have inhibited and impeded their best efforts, especially at the Olympic Games.

Canadian competitors won no gold medals at the winter games in 1936 (Berlin), 1956 (Cortina), 1972 (Sapporo), and 1980 (Lake Placid). As well, Canadians failed to win gold medals at the summer games in 1972 (Munich), and 1976 (Moscow). At these games, Canadians earned silver and bronze medals in good numbers, but not one gold medal.

042. Was there an assassination attempt on the life of Tim Buck?

Tim Buck was the popular leader of the Communist Party of Canada. His actions were found to be in contravention of Section 98 of the Criminal Code (the "seditious conspiracy" clause used to deal with dissidents), and he was serving a five-year sentence in Kingston Penitentiary when a riot broke out. Six shots in three volleys were fired into his cell the night of October 17, 1932. By falling to the floor in time, he was unhurt. Buck was released on November 24, 1934, having served half of his sentence. Tim Buck emerged a hero. Two years later the controversial Section 98 was repealed.

043. Which Russian ballet dancer defected in Toronto?

Mikhail Baryshnikov, a leading dancer with the Kirov Ballet, which was then touring North America, defected on June 30, 1974, following a performance at the O'Keefe Centre in Toronto. He was immediately granted asylum and went on to re-establish his Russian reputation in the capitals of the Western world.

044. Who is the chief Boy Scout in Canada?

By virtue of his office, the chief Boy Scout in Canada is the governor general of Canada. The chief Girl Guide is the wife of the governor general.

045. Who or what was "Mrs. Mike"?

Mrs. Mike was the title of a best-selling biography of Katherine Mary O'Fallon, a high-spirited, sixteen-year-old Boston girl who meets and marries Michael (Mike) Flannigan, a gallant RCMP sergeant with "eyes so blue you could swim in them." He introduces an urban woman to the delights of northern life at Hudson's Hope, Yukon Territory, before the First World War. It was written by two American writers, Benedict and Nancy Freedman, and turned into the movie *Mrs. Mike* (1949), directed by Louis King and starring Dick Powell and Evelyn Keyes.

046. How many Marx brothers were there?

Were there four Marx brothers, or seven, or eleven?

One immediately thinks of the American vaudevillians and movie personalities: Groucho, Harpo, Zeppo, Beppo. But there was also a Canadian family of seven Marx brothers, known as "The Canadian Kings of the Repertoire" from Cape Breton to the Cariboo, according to an article in *Early Canadian Life*, August 1978.

The Canadian Marx brothers were a troupe of entertainers headed by Thomas Sr., a former cobbler from Perth, Ontario, who led his sons — R.W., Joseph, Thomas, Ernie, Alex, John, and McIntyre. Each son had his own specialty, whether song, dance, recitations, sketches, melodrama (villainy versus virtue), slide show, etc. They entered the town with a brass-band parade and ran a "clean" show. It was said that no one ever saw the Marx company twice — "he died laughing."

The Marx Company toured from 1870 to the 1920s, when it came to break up. Thomas Sr. once saw Groucho Marx perform but felt the American comedian's act was not smooth enough!

047. Whose body lay in state in the old Montreal Forum?

The funeral of hockey player Howie Morenz, know as the Stratford Streak, was held in the old Montreal Forum, at centre ice, on March 11, 1937. Fifty thousand people filed past the catafalque, and 250,000 Quebeckers lined the route to the cemetery. It was the most-attended funeral service in Canadian history.

048. Were Ukrainian Canadians mistreated during and following the Great War?

In 1988 the Ukrainian Committee of the Civil Liberties Commission determined that from 1914 to 1920, 8,579 so-called enemy aliens were incarcerated, including women and children. According to Victor Malarek, "Ukrainian Canadians Seeking Redress," the *Globe and Mail*, January 15, 1988, "Of that number, 3,138 could be classified as prisoners of war ... the other 5,441 were civilians ... a further 88,000, most of them Ukrainian, were categorized as enemy aliens and were obliged to report regularly to their local police authorities or to the North West Mounted Police." This was done legally under the War Measures Act of 1914.

049. Who was the witch of Plumb Hollow?

The so-called witch of Plumb Hollow was Mrs. Elizabeth Barnes, a farmer's wife who was known locally as a clairvoyant and fortune teller. She called herself Mother Barnes and was feared yet frequented by members of the farming communities around Plumb Hollow, near Athens, which is near Brockville, Ontario. In 1889 she was sought out by George Dagg, a farmer from Shawville, Quebec, who believed he had a poltergeist on his farm. Blessed with "second sight" and the "sixth sense" (for she claimed to be "the seventh daughter of the seventh daughter"), Mother Barnes identified the cause of the disturbance: an adolescent girl with a troubled psyche. In the process, she inspired at least one novel and a number of short plays. Her abandoned log cabin was still standing in the late 1990s.

050. Who claimed Canada as his personal possession?

Alexander Humphreys claimed Canada as his personal possession. The otherwise-humble schoolmaster made the astonishing claim and came close to proving it in 1839 during an amazing trial in Edinburgh, Scotland.

Humphreys maintained that he was the descendent of Sir William Alexander, who in 1625 and 1628 had been granted land across much of today's Eastern Canada. The direct line of inheritance died out in 1739. Nonetheless, there were two pretenders.

The first claimant was William Alexander Stirling, an American soldier, who tried to claim the title and the immense land grants. But he was unable to prove his legal right to the title.

The second claimant was Alexander Humphreys, the humble schoolmaster, who claimed he was the Earl of Stirling, Hereditary Viceroy of the Canadas, Lord Lieutenant of Nova Scotia, Proprietor of Maine and New Brunswick, Master of the Grand Banks Fisheries, Absolute Owner of All Lands, Waterways, and Minerals found between the Great Lakes and California.

Humphreys supplied documents to prove his claim, but he was in turn accused of imposture and forgery. Losing his case, he settled in Washington, D.C., where he and then his sons continued to press their grandiose claim. *The Man Who Claimed Canada* was the title of a CBC Radio drama broadcast on December 6, 1954. The play was researched and written by R.S. Lambert.

051. Who are the "titans" of the Canadian big business?

Peter C. Newman, the Boswell of members of Canada's business establishment, has focused on the new breed of powerful men, whom he calls "titans." He does this in his book *Titans: How the New Canadian Establishment Seized Power* (1998), which documents the deals and personal lives of such titans as Ted Rogers, Paul Desmarais, Conrad Black, Eddy Cogan, Peter Nygard, Peter Munk, and Thomas d'Aquino.

052. Did L.M. Montgomery base *Anne of Green Gables* on *Rebecca of Sunnybrook Farm*?

L.M. Montgomery's classic novel *Anne of Green Gables* (1908) has surprising parallels with an earlier and even more famous children's book, *Rebecca of Sunnybrook Farm* (1903), the American classic written by Kate Douglas Wiggin. According to scholar David Howes and writer Constance Classen, similarities of plot, description, and dialogue are so obvious that Montgomery, in the writing of her children's book, must have been consciously or unconsciously influenced by Wiggin's writing. As Andy Lamey noted in "Is Anne of Green Gables Really from Sunnybrook Farm?" *National Post*, April 10, 1999, "Both Anne and Rebecca tell the story of a young girl who goes to live with an older couple after one or both of her parents dies."

053. Who is Dudley Do-Right?

Writers Alex Anderson and Jay Ward created the character of Dudley Do-Right — the upright, uptight, and unbright Mountie — as long ago as 1948. It was not until 1961 that the animated character first appeared as a segment of the TV program *The Bullwinkle Show*. Then Dudley had his own series of brief episodes (each four and a half minutes in duration) on ABC-TV in 196970.

The incompetent Dudley was modelled on Nelson Eddy's Mountie character in the movie *Rose Marie*. Inspector Fenwick supervises Dudley in his battle against his arch enemy, Snidely Whiplash, who repeatedly kidnaps Dudley's girlfriend, Nell (the Inspector's daughter), and ties her to railroad tracks. If that weren't proof enough of his villainy, Snidley also has green skin. According to Michael Dawson in *The Mountie: From Dime Novel to Disney* (1998), Ward has described Dudley as "stalwart, clean-living, chaste, dense — and a crashing bore."

054. Who was the strongest man in the world?

Weight-lifting records are made and broken every year. Yet, in downtown Montreal there is a statue raised to "the strongest man in the world." He is the French-Canadian strongman Louis Cyr (1863–1912), whose strength became a legend. Before the sport of weightlifting was developed, he won every challenge match in North America in 1885 and even claimed the world championship in 1892. Three years later, in Boston, he lifted 1,967 kg, believed to be the heaviest weight ever hoisted by a human being.

Harry Houdini, writing in *Miracle Mongers and Their Methods* (1920), had this to say about Cyr: "It is generally conceded that Louis Cyr was, in his best days, the strongest man in the known world at all-round straight lifting. Cyr did not give the impression of being an athlete, nor of a man in training, for he appeared to be over-fat and not particularly muscular; but he made records in lifting which, to the best of my knowledge, no other man has been able to duplicate."

055. Did Jesse James hide in Ontario?

The American outlaw Jesse James was shot by a fellow gang member, Bob Ford, in April 1882. As John Macdonald wrote in "The Traveller," *CARP News*, May 1998, "The story made the headlines around the world, including Princeton, Ont., a small Oxford County village 50 km southwest of Kitchener. Villagers saw the pictures of James and recognized him as a former local resident, a Mr. Richardson. To this day, over a century later, stories persist around Princeton that Jesse James lived there while on the run from U.S. authorities."

It is said that he arrived in the early 1880s and moved into the local hotel. He bought a horse and buggy and was noted for his marksmanship. He courted a local young lady and after their engagement was announced, he made known his plan to buy a farm on Governor's Road, now Highway 2. Thereupon, he vanished, leaving behind his broken-hearted fiancée.

The legend of James's days in Princeton is one of many stories included by Anna Williamson in *History of Princeton* (1967).

056. Where is there a replica of Lester B. Pearson's study?

Upon the death of former Prime Minister Lester B. Pearson in 1972, a replica of his study from his Ottawa home, complete with books, furnishings, and memorabilia, was fitted into Laurier House in Ottawa, as incongruous as it might seem. The result is that Laurier House could be called Liberal House, for it is associated with three prominent Liberal prime ministers of Canada: Sir Wilfrid Laurier, W.L. Mackenzie King, and Lester B. Pearson.

057. Who was the so-called Lone Cowboy?

Aficionados of the art and fiction of the Wild West know the "Lone Cowboy" as Will James — cowboy, bronco-buster, rodeo performer, cattle-rustler, ex-onvict, Hollywood stuntman, illustrator, and storyteller about Western subjects. Curiously, James was not the adventurer's real name, and contrary to the impression he gave, he was not born in the United States, though he did live in the West and his last decades were spent on his ranch at Pryor Creek, Montana.

A French Canadian by birth and background, he was born Ernest Dufault (1892–1942) at Saint-Nazaire, Eastern Townships, Quebec. At the age of seventeen, he headed out to Alberta, where he ran afoul of the RCMP and then crossed the border, eventually spending time in a U.S. prison. Between 1924 and 1942, he wrote and illustrated twenty-four popular Westerns. Two of them, *Smoky* (1933) and *Lone Cowboy* (1934), were made by Hollywood into movies. His rambunctious life became the subject of a NFB documentary titled *Alias Will James* (1988), directed by Jacques Godbout with music supplied by Ian Tyson.

058. Who was Mary Helena Fortune?

Mary Helena Fortune has an imposing name, but one that is appropriate for an unusual woman and an impressive writer. Born Mary Wilson (1833–1910) of Scottish ancestry, in Belfast, Ireland, she was brought to Canada as a child. In 1851 she married Joseph Fortune, a surveyor, and in 1855 they travelled to Australia to join her father, George Wilson, who was working the goldfields.

In colonial Australia she began to write crime fiction under various pseudonyms for a popular Australian Journal, contributing over five hundred detective stories between 1865 and 1908. Her one-book publication was *The Detectives' Album* (1871), possibly the first collection of detective stories published by a woman. She died under mysterious circumstances.

She wrote one of the longest-running series in crime fiction and pioneered the "police procedural." She was probably the first woman to write stories narrated by a police detective, and certainly the first woman to make a literary specialty of crime fiction. These details come from George Vanderburgh, publisher of the reprint edition of *The Detectives' Album: Stories of Crime and Mystery from Colonial Australia* (2002).

059. Did Biggles ever fly North?

Biggles did, although his flight is pretty well forgotten these days.

Biggles is short for Flying Officer James Bigglesworth, the action hero of a series of boys' adventure novels that were published in England between 1932 and 1998 and were read throughout the Empire and the Commonwealth. Biggles's big decade was the 1950s.

In the novels, the intrepid aviator was a dauntless adventure hero born of English stock in India and raised at a school in England. He flew a Sopwith Camel during the Great War, worked with British Intelligence, flew a Spitfire with the RAF during the Second World War, and then sought out adventure in South America, Australia, Asia, Africa, Canada, and behind the Iron Curtain.

Ninety-eight of these thrilling, well-loved novels were published. They were written by Captain William Early Johns (1893–1968), an English writer and former Flying Officer who promoted himself to "Captain" following the success of the early Biggles books. The last in the series is *Biggles Sees Too Much* (1970). In all, Johns wrote close to two hundred works of fiction for young readers, including a series for girls about Joan Worrals, a determined, eighteen-year-old flier for the WAAF during Second World War.

Of specific Canadian interest is the fact that Canadian editions of a number of these novels were published by the Musson Book Company of Toronto. Curiously, one novel that Musson failed to release in Canada is *Biggles Flies North* (1938), in which the flier heads for the Great Northwest in pursuit of villains who lack common decency and are intent upon the subversion of good old British values in the Dominion upon the eve of the Second World War.

060. Who was Canada's "King of the Pulps"?

King of the Pulps, published in 2003, is about H. (for Henry) Bedford-Jones (1887–1949). The three authors of the book (Peter Ruber, Darrell C. Richardson, and Victor A. Berch) explain that, between 1909 and the year of his death, Bedford-Jones wrote 231 novels and 1,141 short stories — some 25 million words published in the American and British pulp magazines, which were then very popular, under his own name and a host of pseudonyms,

The phenomenally prolific "pulpster" was born in Napanee, Ontario, attended one year at Trinity College in Toronto, worked as a newspaperman in the United States, came into his own as a freelancer contributor to the pulps, and spent his last years in Palm Springs, California, where he died.

He wrote fast-moving tales in most of the genres: adventure, fantasy, epic heroism, science fiction, horror, crime, true-crime, westerns, etc. In the 1920s he was described as the highest paid pulp writer in the United States. Today, his tales seem simple-minded, yet there is the thrill of the chase to them.

As Allan Hawkwood, he wrote the "Famous John Solomon Adventure Series" in the 1930s, which was set in the Middle East of the same period. His earliest fiction dealt with New France's *Ancien Régime* and the Northwest fur trade, but he soon found that imaginative adventure tales set in exotic climes sold best. The Depression dealt a death blow to most of the pulps; those that survived were polished off by television and then paperback originals. These originals were a throwback to the earlier penny dreadful and dime novels.

In 1934 H. BedfordJones jokingly ceded the title "King of the pulps" to a friend and fellow writer, Earle Stanley Gardner, the lawyer who created Perry Mason.

061. Who are the country's leading stand-up comedians?

Mark Breslin answered this question in his book, *The Yuk Yuk's Guide to Canadian Stand-up* (2009). A student of comedy, Breslin knows what is funny ... or at least what is comic. It was 1974 when, in Toronto, he founded the Yuk Yuk's chain of comedy clubs, which has sixteen locations across Canada.

He was asked to name the "ten most influential Canadian stand-ups" by Bruce Demara, who published the list in "Breslin a No-brainer for Book," *The Toronto Star*, November 8, 2009. Here is his choice of names, in alphabetical order:

1. Dave Broadfoot.

2. Brent Butt.

3. Jim Carrey.

4. Larry Horowitz.

5. Elvira Kurt.

6. Mike MacDonald.

7. Howie Mandel.

8. Paul Mandell.

9. Russell Peters.

10. Kenny Robinson.

Although these comics are known to write and perform their own material, he leaves off the list those people who are strictly writers or movie and television personalities known for their light comic touches. Among the Canadian performers and contributors to the Second City revues and *Saturday Night Live* are such talented comedians and comic actors as Leslie Nielsen, Bill Murray, Dan Aykroyd, Mike Myers, etc. All of them make Canadians — as well as North Americans — laugh (and sometimes groan!).

062. Who discovered the Calypso borealis?

John Muir discovered and described the Calypso borealis, a rare white orchid that he encountered on his trek across the Holland Marsh, north of Toronto. At the time (1865–66) he was in his mid-twenties and a wanderer, working as a sawmill-hand and living in a log cabin outside Meaford, Ontario. In 1892 he established the Sierra Club to protect the environment.

"The flower was white and made the impression of the utmost simply purity, like a snow flower," he recalled at the age of seventy-one. "It seemed the most spiritual of all the flower people I had ever met. I sat down beside it and fairly cried for joy. It seems wonderful that so frail and lovely a plant has such power over human hearts. This Calypso meeting happened some forty-five years ago, and was more memorable and impressive than any of my meetings with human beings excepting, perhaps, Ralph Waldo Emerson and one or two others."

These details come from Cameron Smith's column "Muir's Long Cabin the Bush," the *Toronto Star*, October 11, 2003.

063. Who was Quebec's "rural cartoonist"?

One of the country's most charming illustrators was Albert Chartier, born and trained in Montreal in 1912, where he worked as a freelance illustrator. "For almost sixty years, from 1943 until 2002, Chartier drew the monthly comic strip *Onésime* for *Le Bulletin des Agriculteurs*, a magazine that, like *The Old Farmer's Almanac*, remains a fixture of rural Québécois life." So wrote Jett Heer, in "Culture High and Low," *National Post*, November 20, 2003.

The central character of his comic strip is Onésime, a chinless, pipe-smoking, Walter Mitty figure of a man who is married to Zéonïde, an opera-going matron. As Heer points out, Chartier's subject is rural attitudes, but his style was as modern and cosmopolitan as the cartoons that appeared in *The New Yorker* of the day.

Chris Oliveros, publisher of *Drawn and Quarterly*, in Volume 5, fall 2003, devoted more than seventy pages to the reproduction and study of Chartier's art, which may be compared and contrasted with that of Jimmy Frise, who at approximately the same time drew "Birdseye Center" for the *Toronto Star Weekly*. Chartier's audience was at once more rural and more sophisticated than Frise's.

064. Was Sir Henry Baskerville a Canadian?

Sir Henry Baskerville is the principal character in Sir Arthur Conan Doyle's novel *The Hound of the Baskervilles* (1902). In the Sherlock Holmes mystery, Sir Henry is an Englishman "who had been farming in Canada until he inherited a baronetcy from his uncle, Sir Charles Baskerville, upon the latter's mysterious death." The location of Sir Henry's farm is unspecified in the novel, but Doyle wrote that he bought his boots in Toronto, from a bootmaker named Meyers. (The "Meyers, Toronto" reference led to the founding of the fan group known as the Bootmakers of Toronto in 1972. At the turn of the century, a shoemaker named Meyers had a shop on Wellington Street in the city. Donald Campbell Meyers was a leading psychiatrist at the turn of the century in Toronto.) He returns to the Moors and is confronted with the mysterious Hound! Further details appear in Christopher Redmond's article "Sherlock Holmes from Sea to Sea" in *Lasting Impressions: The 25th Anniversary of the Bootmakers of Toronto, The Sherlock Holmes Society of Canada* (1997), edited by George A. Vanderburgh.

065. Was Sherlock Holmes a Canadian?

Enthusiasts of the Sherlock Holmes stories enjoy arguing strange theses and proving odd theories, such as the fact that Dr. Watson was five-times married and the suggestion that Holmes was a Canadian. The latter notion stems entirely from the fact that Canadians have the habit of adding "eh?" to the ends of their sentences. Holmes, it seems, uses the construction a number of times, notably in his first adventure, *A Study in Scarlet* (1887), where he says to Watson, "I might not have gone but for you, and so have missed the finest study I ever came across: a study in scarlet, eh?"

066. What is "The Scarlet Claw" all about?

In the Universal Studios movie *The Scarlet Claw* (1944), Basil Rathbone plays Sherlock Holmes and Nigel Bruce appears as Dr. Watson. It is a propaganda film set in Quebec City and the rural village of "La Morte Rouge." As Christopher Redmond wrote in "Sherlock Holmes from Sea to Sea," *Lasting Impressions: The 25th Anniversary of the Bootmakers of Toronto, The Sherlock Holmes Society of Canada* (1997), edited by George A. Vanderburgh:

> Holmes solves a series of murders which are initially being blamed on a monster or a supernatural influence. The film ends with a coy scene in which Holmes and Watson are driving through a forest on the first stage of their journey home to England. Watson says he would like to have seen more of

Canada on the trip, and Holmes agrees, speaking in the style of a civics textbook about Canada's "relations of friendly intimacy with the United States on the one hand and their unswerving fidelity to the British Commonwealth and the motherland on the other. Canada, the link which joins together these great branches of the human family."

The film appeared the year following the first Quebec Conference in September 1943, which saw the meeting between Franklin D. Roosevelt and Winston Churchill.

067. Was Richard Hannay a Canadian?

Richard Hannay is a character in a series of popular thrillers written by the Scots novelist John Buchan. Hannay makes his debut in *The Thirty-nine Steps* (1915) as a South African mining engineer who recently settled in London. In later novels he joins the British Army, rises to the rank of general, and exposes a series of espionage rings, saving England from unspecified enemies on a number of occasions. This Hannay thus has no Canadian connection.

Yet, when Alfred Hitchcock filmed *The 39 Steps* (1935), described as "adapted from the novel by John Buchan," he went out of his way to identify the hero as a Canadian. Hitchcock was assuring himself of a North-American market for the film by transforming an Australian hero into a Canadian one. In one of the film's celebrated vaudeville scenes, Hannay — played by English actor Robert Donat — asks the character Mr. Memory, "How far is it from Winnipeg to Montreal?"

Mr. Memory (played by Wylie Watson) replies, "Ah, a gentleman from Canada. You're welcome, sir. [Applause from the audience.] Winnipeg, the fair city of Canada and the capital of the province of Manitoba. Distance from Montreal? 1,454 miles. Am I right, sir?"

Hannay replies, "Quite right!"

Buchan's novel remains in print to this day and is highly regarded by its readers; however, it is Hitchcock's version of Richard Hannay that most people remember, not specifically as a Canadian, but as an agreeable chap.

068. Who are Ghandl and Skaay and why are they great?

Gandhl and Skaay are the names of two great poets of the Haida people. Their narrative poems would be lost, but were recited in the original Haida language to an anthropologist who transcribed, translated, and annotated them in English. These texts so impressed the British Columbia poet and scholar Robert Bringhurst that he devoted a substantial book to the study of them: *A Story as Sharp as a Knife: the Classical Haida Mythtellers and Their World* (1999). He followed it with *Nine Visits to the Mythworld: Ghandl of the Qayahi Llaanes* (2000) and *Being in Being: the Collected Works of Skaay of the Qquuna Qiighawaay* (2001).

Ghandl of the Qaysun Aqyahl Llaanas was born about 1851 and died about 1920. He was christened Walter McGregor and in later years was blind. In 1900 he dictated his narrative poems to anthropologist and linguist J.R. Swanton, who translated and annotated them with the assistance of a bilingual Haida named Henry Moody.

Of Ghandl, Bringhurst writes, "He seems to me a great deal more accomplished — and therefore far more worthy of celebration as a literary ancestor — than any Canadian poet or novelist who was writing in English or French during his time. In fact I know of no one writing in any language, anywhere in North America toward the end of the nineteenth century, who uses words with greater sensitivity and skill. He seems to me not just an exceptional man ... but a figure of durable importance in the history of literature."

Skaay of the Qquuna Qiighawaay is also known as Robert McKay or John Sky. His vital years were roughly 1827 to 1905, and at some point he was crippled. He also dictated his narrative poems to Swanton in 1900. Bringhurst regards Skaay as "the greatest Haida poet whose work survives."

A typical narrative by Ghandl or Skaay — long and seemingly discursive — relates a tale of archaic creation or everyday event, timeless or temporal, or both together. It might commence with the words "they say" and conclude with the words "this is where it ends" or "so it ends."

Bringhurst regards the nineteenth century as the classic period of Haida expression. His work is a "reclamation project" of cultural interest, though it is unlikely that the general public will ever be in a position to appreciate the quality and interest of the narratives of Ghandl and Skaay and other Haida "mythtellers" — not to mention the "mythtellers" of the other indigenous languages of North America.

069. Who were LaFontaine and Baldwin and why are they important?

Louis-Hippolyte LaFontaine and Robert Baldwin were lawyers and parliamentarians from Montreal and Toronto who, following the Rebellions of 1837, worked against the British administration's attempts to assimilate the French of Upper Canada into the English society of Upper Canada.

LaFontaine and Baldwin formed governments in 1842 and 1848 and had a profound effect on public administration, the legal system, and public education in pre-Confederation Canada. They are remembered as the architects of responsible government. They set the country on the road to democracy, racial amity, and national sovereignty — aims realized two decades later in the 1867 Act of Confederation.

The achievement of LaFontaine and Baldwin's achievement, against such heavy odds, was recalled by John Ralston Saul, author and intellectual, who wrote and lectured on the ability of French and English Canadians to work together to deal with common problems.

Saul was the first speaker in the annual LaFontaine-Baldwin Symposium Lectures in Toronto in 2000, a joint undertaking of Saul and The Dominion Institute. The institute, headed by Rudyard Griffiths, is a national, non-partisan, charitable organization founded in 1997 to promote a better understanding and appreciation of Canadian history. Subsequent speakers included Alain Dubuc (Montreal), Georges Erasmus (Vancouver), and David Malouf (Toronto).

070. Who was the first American president to visit Canada?

It was not until July 1936 that a president of the United States visited Canada. The visit was a private one and the response to the express invitation of John Buchan, Governor General Lord Tweedsmuir. That summer, U.S. president Franklin Delano Roosevelt "took the opportunity of a sailing trip off Nova Scotia with his sons at the end of July to see Buchan in Quebec. Amazingly, it was the first official visit of an American president to Canada."

Buchan and Roosevelt had been friends and admirers for years. Indeed, Buchan had hoped to be appointed Britain's ambassador to the United States instead of governor general of Canada. FDR referred to Tweedsmuir as "the best Governor General Canada ever had."

This information comes from Andrew Lownie's *John Buchan: The Presbyterian Cavalier* (1995). Howard Taft was one of a number of U.S. presidents who recalled youthful vacations and hunting expeditions in Canada before they assumed the mantle of power.

071. What was unusual about Glenn Gould's name and signature?

Glenn Gould's name and signature were quite unusual.

Recipients of letters from the recording artist found that he seldom bothered to write the last letter of his first name. In haste he would sign his letters "Glen Gould." The signature looks odd.

Scholars have noted that at his birth, on September 15, 1932, he was registered "Glenn Herbert Gold." At the time anti-Semitism was a factor in Toronto, and although the family was Presbyterian and not Jewish, family members felt it was wiser to spell the family name "Gould" rather than "Gold" (a name identified with European Jewry).

072. Who are the "top ten" Canadians?

People enjoy making lists and reading them, especially graded lists, which organize one's thoughts on the relative importance of its items. For *The Top Ten Greatest Canadians*, CBC-TV invited members of the public to vote on the "top ten" Canadians of all-time from all walks of life, and a list of fifty names was supplied as a reminder of claims to greatness. On November 29, 2004, the results of the voting were telecast. Here are the top ten in order of popularity:

1. T.C. Douglas, founder of Medicare.

2. Wayne Gretzky, hockey star.

3. Don Cherry, hockey commentator.

4. Sir John A. Macdonald, first prime minister.

5. Terry Fox, marathon runner.

6. Frederick Banting, co-discoverer of insulin.

7. Lester B. Pearson, prime minister and Nobel laureate.

8. Alexander Graham Bell, telephone inventor.

9. David Suzuki, scientist and environmentalist.

10. Pierre Elliott Trudeau, prime minister.

073. What were Beatrice Lillie's fondest memories of her hometown?

In her golden years — between the two world wars — Beatrice Lillie was well-described as "the toast of two continents." She performed in the West End and Broadway and starred in countless touring productions. Called "the ungilded lily," this star of musical comedy was born in Toronto, married to Sir Robert Peel, and was in her early forties when she agreed to be interviewed by R.E. Knowles of the *Toronto Star* (March 31, 1936).

Lillie never hid her background of genteel poverty in Toronto; indeed, she sprinkled it with stardust, at the urging of R.E. Knowles, who encouraged her to reminisce about the early years in the city. He asked her about the things she would like to re-experience, so she strode down Memory Lane:

> Oh, lots of things — I'd love, once more, to go out with my new parasol the first warm day — or to win a race at the Sunday school picnic — or to duck for apples on Hallowe'en — or to cut a swath, on the sidewalk, with my new skipping-rope — or to hear the bell once more when my boy-friend called to take me to a party — or to go to Hanlan's Point and stay till it got quite dark. Or, perhaps most, to have one more long day at the Exhibition — and — and this — to gather in all the "samples" — all free and all beautiful. Ah, me! It's all very fine to imagine all this — but it will never, never, come back again.

Knowles listened and all the while observed her expressive features: "The fine face now aglow with the tender and wistful light that only yesterday can lend."

074. Who was "the real McCoy"?

When something or someone is genuine or bona fide, the folk expression "the real McCoy" is applied. There is no agreement as to the expression's origin, but Canadians have argued that it refers to Elijah McCoy (1843–1929), a black inventor or technician who was born in Colchester, Ontario. According to Barbara Wickens, writing in "Immersed in Canadiana," *Maclean's Special Commemorate Issue 100*, October 2004.

McCoy, the son of escaped slaves from Kentucky, "registered more than fifty patents in his lifetime, including one for a lawn sprinkler, an ironing board, and a train-wheel lubricator that came to be known as 'the real McCoy.'" The lubricator was self-regulating and eliminated the need for trains to come to a full stop for lubrication. The first claim to be "the real McCoy" was made on his behalf only in 1992.

075. Why is Henry Ross honoured in Australia?

It is not often that a foreign government honours a Canadian-born rebel or hero, but the Australian government did so officially when it drew attention to the role played by Henry Ross in the Eureka Stockade standoff, near Ballarat, Southern Australia, on December 3, 1854. The official endorsement came from Canberra exactly 150 years later.

"It was Toronto-born Henry Ross, a twenty-seven-year-old miner who emerged from the historic battle with mortal wounds but an enduring place in Australia's national mythology." So wrote Randy Boswell in "Australia Honours Toronto Rebel," *National Post*, December 3, 2004.

In 1849 Ross joined many other former miners from around the world in the Australian gold rush. He became a leader of the uprising at Ballarat to protest the high licensing fees and the colonial regime's blocking of democratic reforms, including voting rights. He helped to draft the miners' list of demands, a document important in the evolution of responsible government in Australia.

For the miners, Ross even designed a distinctive blue-and-white flag, inspired by the Southern Cross, the four-star constellation visible in the night sky in the southern hemisphere. The image of the constellation was subsequently adopted as a distinctive part of the country's official flag. The original flag is preserved in the museum at Ballarat, the modern city at the site of the Eureka standoff.

As Boswell noted, the raising of the flag was a decisive moment in the colony's history: it was the subject of a watercolour drawn on the spot by a French Canadian named Charles Alphonse Doudiet, a miner and rebel sympathizer. The watercolour depicts the rebels ringed around Ross's flag. A century later the watercolour was discovered in an attic of a descendant. Since then, it has been reproduced in history texts and on Australian stamps. Along with the present-day Australian flag, it draws attention to the enduring contribution of two former Canadians — Ross and Doudiet — to the independence of Australia, Canada's "sister Dominion."

076. How many federal ministers have resigned from Cabinet on principle?

There is much talk of "ministerial responsibility," but in the last sixty or so years, of the hundreds of members of Parliament who have been appointed to federal Cabinet posts, only two ministers have ever resigned from Cabinet on matters of principle.

Columnist Graham Fraser made this observation in his article "Missile Defence Debate Haunts P.M.," the *Toronto Star*, December 19, 2004. He noted that James L. Ralston, minister of national defence in Prime Minister Mackenzie King's Cabinet, resigned in 1942 over the issue of conscription. (King opposed conscription, Ralston favoured it.) It was not until 1963 that the second Cabinet minister, another minister of national defence, resigned. Douglas Harkness left Cabinet to protest Prime Minister John G. Diefenbaker's refusal to accept arming Canada's Bomarc missiles with nuclear warheads. The first resignation occurred during the Second World War, and the second at the height of the Cold War.

077. Do New Canadians receive free Bibles?

Free copies of the King James version of the Bible were automatically presented to all new Canadians at citizenship ceremonies for a period of about fifty years. Copies were made available on a complimentary basis by the Canadian Bible Society. The practice of such presentations was discontinued in 1998 in the interests of multiculturalism, freedom of religion, and a separation of church and state.

The Bible Society objected. According to Leslie Scrivener, in "Welcome to Canada: Bring Your Own Bible," the *Toronto Star*, December 26, 2004: "We are very concerned that this is not protecting the rights of Canadians — it's taking away rights. If you exclude something how are you protecting people's freedom? What if most people want them?"

Removal of the Bibles was supported by the Humanist Association of Canada, which recommended that the oath of allegiance should be based on a non-religious statement. Its director noted, "When you give testimony is your religious faith relevant? What is important is your obligation to fellow citizens and your country to tell the truth."

078. Who was Whipper Billy Watson?

Fans of wrestling enjoyed watching the astounding feats and dumb-founding deeds of Whipper Billy Watson (1916–1990), the country's best-known professional wrestler. He was born William Potts in Toronto. Until his retirement, following an automobile accident in 1971, he brought colour to the ring and won numerous titles, including the world wrestling and the commonwealth championships. It is said that he won 99 percent of the 6,300 matches in his thirty-year career. He is fondly remembered by fans for the Canadian Avalanche (cartwheels that dazzled opponents) and Canuck Commando Unconscious (a special grip that momentarily puts an opponent out of commission). In retirement he assisted charities for impaired children and the disabled. As for his nickname, it is said that he "whipped" all his opponents.

079. How many serving prime ministers have had to testify in court?

It is extremely rare for a prime minister still in office to testify before a court of law. More often, a former prime minister is required to appear in court to offer testimony about government procedures and policies.

While still in office, two Canadian prime ministers were summoned to appeared before judges.

Prime Minister John A. Macdonald appeared before a three-man commission on September 17, 1873, to explain his involvement (or non-involvement) in the Pacific Scandal. He was accused of soliciting election funds from Sir Hugh Allan in exchange for Allan's appointment to the presidency of the Canadian Pacific Railway Company. Macdonald claimed, "These hands are clean!" but the commission found him guilty of "having obtained money from a suspicious source and having applied it to illegitimate purposes." He subsequently resigned from office to sit in the Opposition benches. Throughout, Macdonald wrapped himself in the flag of Canadian nationalism.

Prime Minister Paul Martin appeared on February 10, 2005, before the Gomery Commission, which investigated the expenditure of public funds that had been awarded largely without tender or accountability to Liberal-friendly advertising agencies in Quebec. The prime minister at the time was Jean Chrétien, and he appeared as a witness. Paul Martin, his minister of finance and subsequently his successor as prime minister, testified that he knew nothing of what had happened. In fact, both Chrétien and Martin wrapped themselves in the flag of Canadian unity.

080. Do portraits of living Canadians appear on postage stamps?

By tradition, portraits of living Canadians do not appear on Canadian postage stamps. However, regular-issue stamps do bear likeness of the reigning monarchs, and since Her Majesty Queen Elizabeth II is a Canadian by statute, her portrait does appear on stamps. At the same time, some commemorative stamps bear recognizable images of living hockey stars and astronauts, but these are issued to mark group endeavours. Canada Post broke its tradition with the issue of a stamp that bears the beaming features of jazz pianist Oscar Peterson. The 50-cent stamp appeared on August 15, 2005, to celebrate his eightieth birthday and mark Peterson's contribution to the world of popular music.

081. Did a Canadian play a role in Lincoln's assassination?

In a way, a man of Canadian birth did play a part in that assassination.

During the American Civil War, U.S. president Abraham Lincoln, while attending a production at Ford's Theatre in Washington, was shot and mortally wounded by John Wilkes Booth, actor and Confederate agent. Booth, ever theatrical, leapt onto the stage and yelled to the horrified audience, "Sic semper tyrannis!" before making his escape.

The assassination occurred on April 14, 1865. The plot on Lincoln's life had been hatched by Confederate sympathizers who had met earlier in a Montreal hotel. Booth was identified as the gunman and hunted down by Union troops. Twelve days later, on April 26, they cornered him and he was shot dead by a Union officer, Lieutenant Edward P. Doherty. As it happened, Doherty was a native of London in present-day Ontario. "He received a $5,000 reward for his act," explained Claire Hoy in his study *Canadians in the Civil War* (2005).

082. Was Uncle Tom a Canadian?

Yes and no. Uncle Tom is the literary character created by the American author Harriet Beecher Stowe in her famous and influential novel *Uncle Tom's Cabin* (1852), which is credited with turning public sentiment against slavery in the United States. Admired by Leo Tolstoy and other great humanitarians, the novel is engrossing literature with a message. Uncle Tom is a appealing family man who manages to make good his escape from bondage in the Deep South and find freedom "across the line" in British North America.

Stowe modelled Uncle Tom on the real Josiah Henson, a former American whose own story, in memoir form, was published in 1849. Henson, a slave in Maryland, was separated from his parents, twice sold, continually beaten, and maimed for life. As Wayne Kelly explains in "Inside Uncle Tom's Cabin," *Heritage Matters* (Ontario Heritage Foundation), March 2005:

In 1829, Henson arranged to purchase his freedom with money he earned by preaching to Methodist congregations. Betrayed by his master, Henson was taken to New Orleans to be sold. Henson escaped slavery by fleeing northwards with his wife Nancy and four children using the Underground Railroad, eventually crossing the Niagara River into Upper Canada (now Ontario) on October 18, 1830.

In Upper Canada, Henson worked as a farm labourer and lay preacher. Then he teamed up with anti-slavery advocates who acquired 200 acres in Dawn Township in southern Ontario near Dresden, where, in 1836, they established a "settlement" for fugitives from slavery. The community expanded and eventually attracted some five hundred settlers. After three or so decades, it was phased out, with many former slaves returning to the United States or fanning out across Canada.

Visitors to the area may tour Uncle Tom's Cabin Historic Site, which will be found on a bend in the Sydenham River, near the town of Dresden. The log cabin dates from 1841 and is furnished in the manner of the times. For a century the words "Uncle Tom" stood for the stoical benevolence of a people, except in the United States during the 1960s, when Black activists felt it was a condescending reference to "a good Negro" — someone who "knew his place." But in all the ways that are important, Uncle Tom, Josiah Henson, Canadian, was a good and just man and serves as a model for all men. Because of his own actions and because of the artistry of Harriet Beecher Stowe, his name continues to be synonymous with freedom from servitude.

083. Who is the sole non-physician commemorated by the CMC?

The sole non-physician to be commemorated by the Canadian Medical Association is T.C. (Tommy) Douglas (1904–1986). In October 1998, a dozen years after his death, he was inducted into the CMC's Hall of Fame as the "Father of Medicare." The citation noted, "His leadership has provided long-term benefits to medical science in Canada, and a Canadian health-care system [that is] a source of envy to other countries." The citation failed to mention the fact that in 1962 the CMC attempted to block the implementation of the form of medical insurance introduced by Tommy Douglas, first in Saskatchewan and then across the country. The irony of this was noted by Ed Finn in "The Father of Medicare," *The CCPA Monitor*, February 2005.

084. Was Jack the Ripper a Canadian?

Too much time has passed for the identity of the serial murderer known as Jack the Ripper to be determined, but theories abound.

Who could be responsible? To have murdered and dismembered a series of London prostitutes in surgical fashion required a certain profile, and Francis J. Tumblety is a good candidate. The son of an immigrant Irishman, Tumblety was *probably* born in 1833, *likely* in present-day Ontario or Quebec. He was raised, however, in Rochester, New York, and Detroit, Michigan. He practised a form of medicine in Montreal and Saint John, New Brunswick (in the 1850s, medical practices was largely unregulated). He eventually turned up in London, and on November 7, 1888 was charged with homosexual offences; the actual murders had been taking place since August of that year.

Five days following Tumblety's arrest, Scotland Yard considered him a suspect in the Whitehall murders because he possessed anatomical knowledge and was suspected of being a hater of "womankind." He was allowed to post bail on November 24 and thereafter he fled to France. No reports of murders with mutilations in Whitechapel were made during and following his period of imprisonment. Eventually, he turned up in New York City, lived in St. Louis, and later died a wealthy man, in 1903.

Was he Jack the Ripper? Could be. These details come from Massimo Polidoro's article "Was a Quack Doctor Jack the Ripper," *Skeptical Inquirer*, March-April 2005. Polidoro's research is based on the study *Jack the Ripper: First American Serial Killer* (1996), written by Stewart Evans and Paul Gainey.

085. Who said, "Canada 6, Russia 5?"

That was the score of the final hockey game of the Team Canada–USSR Summit Series on Moscow ice on September 28, 1972. Paul Henderson's overtime goal brought the closely fought series to a fitting close! The words themselves are associated with the classical actor William Hutt.

Hutt was playing the lead in a *King Lear* matinee performance for students, at the Stratford Festival. According to Richard Ouzounian, writing in "Taking a Final Bow," the *Toronto Star*, April 10, 2005, "Hutt sensed the audience would all rather be elsewhere, but he soldiered bravely ahead as the mad king. Just before the famous storm sequence, Hutt heard in the wings that Paul Henderson had scored the decisive goal. He played through the scene with full passion, then, at the conclusion, turned to the people and simply said, 'Canada 6, Russia 5.' The crowd went wild."

William Hutt's impromptu remark is now enshrined in hockey fame and theatre history.

086. Who is regarded as the Father of Chiropractic?

As unlikely as it might seem, the man who is regarded as the Father of Chiropractic — the single person responsible for promoting and codifying the procedure of spinal manipulation to cure man's ails — was Ontario-born Daniel David Palmer (1845–1913). In 1946 a bronze bust of Palmer, which identifies him as the first practitioner, was erected in Palmer Park in Port Perry, Ontario.

Palmer was raised in this small community north of Oshawa, having been born in the close-by hamlet of Brown's Corners, now known as Audley, part of the community of Ajax. As a twenty-year-old, he joined his family, which had earlier settled in Davenport, Iowa. Palmer practised as a "magnetic healer" and at one point was jailed for practising medicine without a licence. He wrote that he discovered the power of spinal manipulation by restoring the hearing to a long-deaf janitor through the adjustment of a vertebra back into its proper spinal position. He named the process *chiropractic*, Latin for "done by hand."

In *The Chiropractor's Adjuster* (1910), he wrote, "It was I who combined the science and art and developed the principles thereof. I have answered the time-worn question — what is life?" A photograph of his bust appears in Jim Wilkes's "Facts on Figures," the *Toronto Star*, April 22, 2005.

087. Who won a special Academy Award for choreography in 1969?

Lists of Canadians — both former and new — who have been honoured by the Motion Picture Academy of Arts and Sciences with Academy Awards (or Oscars) invariably omit the special award given to Onna White. Even Canadians forget she was born in this country.

Onna White was born on March 24, 1922, at Inverness, Nova Scotia. She fell in love with dance and moved to the United States, where she performed with the San Francisco Opera Ballet and then in Broadway musicals, first as a dancer and then (at the urging of her mentor Michael Kidd) as a choreographer. She first appeared on Broadway in *Finian's Rainbow* in 1948; she last choreographed for the revival of *Mame* in 1963. She was nominated for eight Tony Awards but won none. Her choreographic talent for intricate dance steps and sequences were used to great effect in Hollywood musicals, outstandingly for *Oliver!* It earned the Best Picture Oscar for 1969, and for her work on that musical she was awarded an honorary Academy Award — Oscars are irregularly awarded for choreography. She joined the likes of Gene Kelly, Jerome Robbins, and her mentor Michael Kidd. It is not recorded whether or not Gaelic dance steps inspired her during her youth on Cape Breton Island.

088. Who is — or was — the world's fastest human?

Ben Johnson has been described as the world's fastest human. The Jamaican-born Canadian runner completed the 100-metre race at the Seoul Olympics on Monday, September 26, 1988. He did so in 9.79 seconds and set the world record. Three days later Olympic officials stripped him of his Gold Medal as they found him guilty of injecting outlawed steroids. They then awarded the medal to his arch-rival, U.S. runner Carl Lewis.

As tends to be the case with records of any sort, eventually Johnson's scandalous 9.79 seconds was bested. Usain Bolt of Jamaica set the current 9.58-second record in 2009.

089. Who is Our Lady of Combermere?

Our Lady of Combermere is a reference to what has been called "the newest shrine in Christendom and the humblest and least pretentious." The history of the shrine and the story of the statue of the Virgin Mary known by that name are especially interesting, because they involve a remarkable Roman Catholic woman by the name of Catherine de Hueck Doherty (1896–1985).

She was born into a devout Orthodox family in Russia and at an early age was married to a baron. Following the Russian Revolution, they moved to England, and then in 1921 she settled in Canada. Here, she worked with Catholic priests and laity among the poor in Toronto, establishing what later came to be recognized as the "lay apostolate." Social problems in New York's Harlem beckoned her, and there she established a Friendship House in 1938. Her marriage annulled, she married again, and the couple settled in Combermere, a small Ontario town in the Diocese of Pembroke, where they established a training centre for Catholic laity. It was named Madonna House in 1954, and there they began to offer summer courses, vocational training, retreats, lectures, and work for volunteer guests. Before long the centre attracted over 200 laymen, women, and priests; "field houses" (regarded as "rooms of Madonna House") were established elsewhere in the country and the world.

Madonna House was formally opened and dedicated to the Virgin Mary on June 8, 1960. Its centrepiece was the statue of Our Lady of Combermere, a bronze, larger-than-life sculpture that depicts the Virgin Mary with open arms and a swirling cape. It is the work of Frances Rich, a sculptress from Santa Barbara, California.

Mrs. Doherty became internationally known for her devotion to living the life of the Gospel. "Nothing is foreign to the Apostolate except sin," she said more than once. She lectured on *poustinia* (Russian for "desert" where real values are encountered) and *sobornost* (unity of heart and mind). Other statements of hers include: "Faith sees God's face in every human face" and "To burn, to love, to share the pain, / This is my life, my song, and its refrain." She is remembered as a pioneer of interracial and social justice. There is a movement among the Roman Catholic laity to have the Vatican recognize her as a candidate for canonization.

090. Who designed the official flag of Newfoundland and Labrador?

The artist Christopher Pratt designed the official flag of Newfoundland and Labrador, and it was adopted by the provincial legislature in 1980. It is described in *Symbols of Heritage* (published by the Department of Canadian Heritage in 2002) in these terms: "Its white area symbolizes snow and ice; blue, the sea; red, human effort; and gold, confidence in the future. The image of the trident (three-pronged spear) on the left side of the flag emphasizes the province's dependence on fishing and the sea. The two red triangles on the right stand for the mainland and island parts of the province, and the golden arrow represents hope for the future." Christopher Pratt has given it a memorable, modern-day appearance.

091. How many Canadians have travelled aboard the Starship *Enterprise*?

The USS *Enterprise* is unquestionably the best-loved starship of all time. It ventures into deep space, battling the Klingons and other menacing forces with every rerun of the original *Star Trek* television series, as well as the movies based on them. Crew members are not identified by nationality, so viewers accept them as citizens of the United States of America in the future.

The nationalities of the actors is incidental to the action, yet the Canadian media has always dwelt on the fact that Commander James T. Kirk is played by veteran actor William Shatner (born 1931) and that chief engineer Lieutenant-Commander Montgomery Scott, invariably known as Scotty, is played with gritty gusto by James Doohan (1920–2005). They were both Toronto-trained radio and stage actors. Shatner was born in Montreal, while Doohan was a native of Vancouver was and raised in Sarnia, Ontario. His death in California occasioned reams of copy and reminiscence. After all, he was *the* Scotty who operated the integrator/disintegrator made memorable by the command, "Beam me up, Scotty!" Fans of the show assure non-fans that the order was never issued in those words in any of the episodes, but popular imagination is stronger than the scripts. So, in answer to the question posed above, two Canadians travelled aboard the Starship *Enterprise*.

092. Who introduced sound to the movies?

Hollywood's first sound feature film, released in the fall of 1927, was *The Jazz Singer* starring Al Jolson. Charles Foster, film historian, claims the technical honours for this achievement could be awarded to three people in Hollywood at the time. There is Jack Warner, head of Warner Brothers, which released Al Jolson's movie; Louis B. Mayer, head of Metro-Goldwyn-Mayer, maintained that Douglas Shearer, sound specialist in his employ, laid the groundwork; and Director Allan Dwan, ahead of Warner and *The Jazz Singer*, filmed a newsreel with sound for Movietone News in the summer of 1927.

As Foster points out, all the contributors were Canadians, sound Canadians!

093. Who is the Canadian-born dancer whose photograph appears on the Beatles' *Sgt. Pepper's* album?

That's a tough question unless you've read Charles Foster's well-researched study titled *Once Upon a Time in Paradise: Canadians in the Golden Age of Hollywood* (2003). When the Beatles released their *Sgt. Pepper's Lonely Hearts Club Band* album in June 1967, no one was more surprised to find his photograph included in the busy collage of the album's cover than child star Bobby Breen. Born in 1927 in Montreal and raised in Toronto, he was an appealing youngster who could sing, dance, and act. Once his talent was discovered, he rode the wave of Hollywood's interest in child stars during the Depression and war years, appearing in such movies as *Let's Sing Again* (1936) with Eddie Cantor and *Hawaii Calls* (1938) with Canadian-born comic actor Ned Sparks. He remains an entertainer to this day, still wondering why the art director of the Beatles album included him among occultist Aleister Crowley and other notables.

094. Are there women who are symbolic of Canada?

Yes and no. The symbol of France is the maiden Marianne; the United States reveres its Statue of Liberty, coincidentally a gift of the French Republic. Canada has boasted two male figures — Johnny Canuck and the Mountie — but no representative women. Yet, some female figures both imaginary and real are so popular they might be said to represent aspects or parts of the country:

- "The Spirit of Canada" is the name of the statue of the draped, mourning woman that stands on the dais of the Canadian

National Vimy Memorial in France. It was sculpted by Walter Aylward and represents grieving motherhood.

- Anne Shirley of Green Gables fame is certainly regarded as the epitome of innocence and virtue as well as the spirit of adventure throughout the Province of Prince Edward Island.

- Evangeline, the victim of the forced evacuation of the Acadians from their land and the heroine of Wordsworth's narrative poem, is honoured in the Province of New Brunswick.

- St. Anne, the mother of the Blessed Virgin Mary, is held in high esteem — as is Mary herself — in the province of Quebec. Indeed, among Roman Catholics, St. Anne is regarded as the patron saint of Canada.

- Laura Secord, the heroine of the War of 1812, is regarded as a hold-out against Yankee aggression, at least in the Niagara Peninsula of the province of Ontario.

As for Western Canada, a number of women are acclaimed for their pioneering spirit or for affirming their constitutional rights. Julie Lagimodière, the mother of Louis Riel, is a justly celebrated Métis settler. Susanna of the Mounties, heroine of four of the novels for young people written by Muriel Denison's, is of interest. Artist and writer Emily Carr and Margaret (Ma) Murray of "the newspapering Murrays" are celebrated right across Canada.

095. Who or what is *The Brooding Soldier?*

The Brooding Soldier is the name of a Canadian war memorial erected at St. Julien, between Ypres and Bruges, Belgium. The combatant depicted has no name because he stands for every soldier. Once seen, the image is never forgotten. It is so mournful, it is sometimes referred to as "The Brooding Canadian." The image has been described as "one of the most striking of all the battlefield memorials on the Western

Front." It stands like a sentinel over those the burial places of those combatants who died during the heroic stand of Canadians during the first gas attack of the First World War.

It is a great shaft of granite which rises 11 metres (35 feet) above a stone-flagged court. Carved into the granite is the unforgettable image of the bowed head and shoulders of a Canadian soldier, with his folded hands resting on arms reversed. "The expression on the face beneath the steel helmet is resolute yet sympathetic, as though its owner meditates on the battle in which his comrades displayed such great valour," according to the wording of the official website sponsored by Veterans Affairs Canada.

The memorial was designed by Frederick Chapman Clemesha, a sculptor from Regina who was wounded while serving with the Canadian Corps during the war. The design was submitted to the competition for the Canadian National Vimy Memorial. It was unveiled on July 8, 1923. The site marks the battlefield where 18,000 Canadians withstood the first German gas attacks of April 22 to 24, 1915. Over 6,000 Canadians died during forty-eight hours of battle. This battle marked the first appearance of Canadians in the European theatre of war. There is much to brood over.

096. Who was dubbed "the Gov'nor" by Frank Sinatra?

Frank Sinatra bestowed nicknames on people whose character, talent, and ability he admired. In London in 1962, he recorded one album with Robert Farnon titled *Great Songs from Great Britain*. Sinatra was so impressed with Farnon's work as composer-conductor-arranger that he dubbed him "the Gov'nor." Their album, released by Decca Records, was no notable contribution to Sinatra's career, but it did affirm Farnon's character, talent, and ability as a composer and arranger of what the British call "light music."

Robert Farnon (1917–2005), born in Toronto, composed for CBC Radio's *The Happy Gang* and then assisted American conductors Paul Whiteman and Andrei Kostelanetz. During the Second World

War, he conducted the Band of the Allied Expeditionary Forces. In the postwar period, he settled in England and composed symphonies, concertos, scores and themes, as well as orchestral arrangements for films and television programs.

097. Were the Smith Brothers Canadian?

According to Bill Casselman's delightful book *Casselman's Canadian Words: a Comic Browse through Words and Folk Sayings Invented by Canadians* (1995): "Smith Brothers cough drops are throat soothers invented by a restaurant owner in St. Armand, Québec, one James Smith. After his death, when his two sons William and Andrew took over the cough drop business, they put engravings of their own bearded selves on the box as a trademark. Many suckers of cough drops thought the two hirsute worthies were inventions of an advertising artist, and that their names were Trade and Mark."

098. Who was A.R. Kaufman?

A.R. Kaufman (1886–1979), the owner of Kaufman Rubber Company in Kitchener, Ontario, was a man with a social conscience. In 1929 he helped to found the Parents' Information Bureau, which trained social workers to make house calls in poor areas to distribute family planning information, including instructions for the use of condoms. At the time, the work of the Bureau was derided and impeded; in the Eastview (Ottawa) Case, the Ontario government brought charges against at least one of its representatives for disseminating birth-control information and offering free contraceptives, but the charges were dismissed by the judge who decided that by such actions the "public good was served." In its day the bureau met the needs of 235,000 mothers.

099. Who were the Canadian Volunteers?

The Canadian Volunteers was the unofficial name of a company formed of members of the Canadian militia who deserted to join the American army when it occupied York (the future Toronto) during the War of 1812. The Stars and Stripes flag was hoisted in York and in distant Newmarket. The Canadian Volunteers, under the command of a disaffected patriot named Joseph Willcocks, led in the destruction of the town of Niagara-on-the-Lake and invaded Fort Erie.

100. Who was the first person to benefit from insulin?

Leonard Thompson was the first person in the world to benefit from the treatment of diabetes with insulin. Leonard was facing imminent death when Dr. Frederick Banting persuaded the thirteen-year-old youngster's parents to agree to an experimental treatment that might prolong his life. The afternoon of January 11, 1922, at the Toronto General Hospital, Leonard was injected with 15 cc of the extract — now known as insulin — devised by Dr. Banting. There was an immediate, observable improvement that was subsequently dubbed "the resurrection effect." Leonard's condition improved dramatically. Through repeated injections, his health was stabilized. Leonard defied all the odds and was alive and well some thirty years after the experimental treatment.

101. Who is Mahmoud Mohammad Issa Mohammad?

Mahmoud Mohammad Issa Mohammad is the name of a convicted Palestinian terrorist who participated in the attack on an El Al jetliner at Athens in December 1968. He boasted of his deed in the book *Je Suis un Fadayim (I Am a Freedom Fighter)* published that year.

Sentenced to seventeen years in prison for this crime, he served only nineteen months, when he was released in an exchange of prisoners. He failed to disclose his criminal record when he entered Canada as a landed immigrant in February 1987 and was living in Brantford, Ontario, when he was apprehended by the Canadian authorities. He has yet to be deported from Canada. His present whereabouts is not publicly known.

102. Could an American citizen become the prime minister of Canada?

According to the Canada Elections Act, only a member of Parliament can serve as the prime minister of Canada. An MP must be a Canadian citizen. However, the Canadian citizen could be either natural-born or naturalized; hence, it is theoretically possible for a naturalized Canadian to hold "dual citizenship" and be recognized as both a citizen of the United States and Canada. While only a natural-born American may serve as an American president, it seems that a dual American-Canadian citizen could serve as the prime minister of Canada.

103. Who were the "twenty-one millionaires"?

The twenty-one millionaires were the wealthy merchants of Newfoundland whose offices and businesses were located on Water Street, the business section of St. John's. In the 1940s, newspaperman and future premier Joey Smallwood maintained that the "twenty-one millionaires" or "Water Street millionaires" controlled Newfoundland's Commission of Government, kept the Newfoundland people in poverty, and resisted his attempts to further union with Canada.

Here is what Harold Horwood has to say about these phantom presences in his lively biography *Joey* (1989): "Those millionaires were another of his inventions. He had decided on twenty-one as a nice, convincing figure. No one really knew how many of the Water

Street merchants were millionaires, but no one ever challenged Joey's statement. The twenty-one pre-confederate millionaires became a fixed part of Newfoundland mythology. (By the time Joey got around to writing his political memoirs in the 1970s, he had forgotten the figure himself, and reduced the millionaires to twenty.)"

104. Who are the "heirs of Lord Durham"?

All Canadians are the "heirs of Lord Durham" in the sense that all Canadians, whether French or English, resident in the country or not, must deal with the radical, reckless, or reasonable notion (take your pick!) that Lord Durham set forth in his *Report on the Affairs of British North America* (1839). The notion was that the French should assimilate to better their lot in life, and it was popularized in *The Heirs of Lord Durham: The Francophones Outside Quebec Speak Out — Manifesto of a Vanishing People* (1978), a report issued by the Canadian Council of Christians and Jews. As historian Ramsay Cook wrote in its Introduction, "French Canadians ... are the heirs to Lord Durham in that they have lived the last one hundred and forty years under the constant threat of assimilation." He concluded, "We are then, French and English Canadians alike, the heirs to Lord Durham. If Canada is ever to become a place where French and English Canadians can live in full harmony, recognizing the validity of each other's culture, then Lord Durham will have to become a genuinely historical figure."

105. Who was the first English-Canadian playwright?

Let me offer the name Barnabas Bidwell, whose play *The Mercenary Match: A Tragedy* was performed by the students of Yale College.

Bidwell was born in Tyringham (now Monterey), Massachusetts, in 1763; he died in Kingston, present-day Ontario, in 1833. While still in the United States, Bidwell graduated from Yale University, served as attorney general of Massachusetts and then as a member of the U.S. Congress. In the words of one commentator, "His residence in Canada resulted from his responsibility for some irregularity in his business as a banker." *The Mercenary Match* was published in New Haven, Connecticut, in 1785. In Upper Canada, Bidwell was known for his reformist sentiments and for his involvement in the Rebellion of 1837, but not as a playwright.

106. Did a Canadian reporter photograph the Kennedy assassination?

The story persists that a Canadian photographer, who found himself in Dallas on the fatal day when U.S. President Kennedy was assassinated (November 22, 1963), took a photograph that clearly shows two assassins in the window of the Texas School Book Depository.

According to Peter Spohn, in "Canadian Was Accidental Witness to History," the *Toronto Star*, November 22, 1998, the photographer was Toronto trade reporter Norman Similas. Now a resident of Richmond Hill, Ontario, Similas is the only Canadian who is known to have witnessed the president's assassination.

Seconds after the shooting, Similas turned his camera onto the depository, though he "was not sure that's where the shots came from." He took six pictures, sped back to his hotel room, and phoned an editor at *The Toronto Star* to confirm the news-wire story. Spohn continued, "The Dallas airport was sealed off, so Similas caught a bus to St. Louis, then a flight to Toronto — via Chicago — to get home. Word was spreading fast that Similas had film of the assassination, and that earned him a motorcycle escort to downtown Chicago, where the film was developed. In Toronto, Similas showed his negatives of the depository to a man claiming to be a *Toronto Telegram* reporter camped outside his Willowdale home."

Similas recalled, "He held my negative up to the light, and said, 'Jesus, there's two guys in the window.'" The window was the one from which Lee Harvey Oswald, the "lone gunman," fired his high-powered rifle. The negative that showed the two figures handling a gun-shaped object was taken "immediately after" the shooting, Similas said.

According to Spohn, "He let the reporter leave with six negatives, all of which were subsequently 'lost.'" An interesting coincidence, considering, as Similas believes, "the one showing two figures was one of the most important negatives taken in this century.'" The RCMP interviewed the reporter, who later denied he saw the two figures.

So who knows?

107. Was the Book-of-the-Month Club (BMOC) founded by a Canadian?

The Book-of-the-Month Club was founded by Harry Scherman (1887–1969), who, though born in Montreal, was raised from the age of two in Philadelphia. He became an advertising copy writer and then a merchandiser and marketer in New York City, producing booklets in the "Little Leather Library" in 1916 to be used as premiums (bonuses for purchasing a product) and then as items for sale through the Woolworth's chain.

Scherman conceived the idea of the Book-of-the-Month Club with publishing executive Robert K. Haas. In April 1926 they sent 4,570 club subscribers, called "members," their first ordered book, known as the "main selection." By year's end the subscriber list had grown to 46,539 members. Even during the Depression, people bought mail-order books at regular prices with the enticement of premiums. The success of this book merchandising operation launched competitors like the Literary Guild. Shares in BOMC were first publicly traded in 1947.

Scherman had two special touches. The first was the "committee of selection," which was established to ensure a balance between cultural and commercial concerns. Its original members were Henry Canby, Dorothy Canfield Fisher, Heywood Broun, Christopher Morley, and William Allen White — well-known literary figures in their day. Scherman's second fine touch was the principle of "negative-option" billing, whereby a subscriber automatically receives next month's "main selection" (with invoice) unless they return a special notice by post before a given date.

Scherman wrote books on economics, inflation, and democracy; he spoke widely on public issues; and he engaged in numerous philanthropies, including serving as director of the MacDowell Colony, the famed writer's retreat.

Canadians subscribed to BOMC from its earliest years. In 1976 the company, establishing a branch operation in Montreal, began to offer Canadian members a limited selection of Canadian titles. A point of interest: Mordecai Richler joined the American "committee of selection."

The Canadian offerings were reduced in scale the 1980s and eventually ended in 1999.

108. Who learned he was the recipient of the 1971 Nobel Prize in Chemistry while sitting alone on the Moscow Express train, which was late leaving the Leningrad Railway Station?

The chemist Gerhard Herzberg (1904–1999) was approached in his cabin on the train by a breathless man, who removed his fur hat, stood at attendance, and said, "Professor Herzberg, I am the secretary of the Soviet Academy of Science, and I have the honour to report that you have been awarded the Nobel Prize in Chemistry." The secretary was responsible for delaying the train's departure so that he could deliver the welcome news.

This is the first incident described by physicist Boris Stoicheff in his biography, *Gerhard Herzberg: An Illustrious Life in Science* (2002). As he explains, the German-born, Canadian chemist of the National Research Council of Canada was travelling alone at the time. His fellow passengers spoke only Russian. Herzberg could only smile to himself for six hours. Herzberg was a world authority on molecular structures, founder of the NRC's spectroscopy laboratory in Ottawa, and the author of "the classic trilogy" of *Molecular Spectra and Molecular Structure*, *Atomic Spectra*, and *Atomic Structure*, which have influenced generations of scientists.

109. Why did the Maple Leaf flag fly at half-staff from the Peace Tower of the Parliament Buildings on March 3, 1999?

The Maple Leaf flag was lowered to half-staff — a unique distinction — to mark the death of the distinguished chemist and physicist Gerhard Herzberg (1904–1999) at his home in Ottawa. The 1991 Nobel laureate in Chemistry, Herzberg established the world-renowned Spectroscopy Laboratory at the National Research Council in Ottawa.

110. What is some of the lore of The Maple Leaf flag?

Here are some facts about the national flag of Canada that are barely known. The flag was first flown on Parliament Hill in Ottawa on February 15, 1965.

1. Its description in English is "National Flag of Canada (Maple Leaf)."

2. Its description in French is "*Drapeau du Canada (l'Unifolié)*." The latter word means "one-leafed."

3. It is possible to imagine, in the top-quarters, the profiles of two long-nosed men glaring into the centre of the Maple Leaf. These men have been nicknamed "Jack" and "Jacques" but are popularly identified with the flag's proponent, Lester B. Pearson, and its opponent, John G. Diefenbaker.

4. If you stare under a bright light at a stationery image of the Maple Leaf for some time (say, thirty seconds), you will see a halo surrounding the leaf.

5. Upside-down, the Maple Leaf bears some resemblance to a fly-swatter or a kitchen spatula.

6. The flag's colours (red and white) are identified with England, and exclude the traditional colour of Quebec (blue), found on that province's fleur-de-lys flag.

7. One reason former prime minister John G. Diefenbaker objected strenuously to the adoption of this particular design was his conviction that schoolchildren would confuse it with the flag of Peru. There are no recorded instances of this ever happening.

8. Here are two detailed descriptions: "A vertical bicolour triband of red, white, and red, with a red maple leaf charged in the centre," and a "Gules on a Canadian pale argent a maple leaf of the first."

111. Is it Maple Leafs or Maple Leaves?

Why is the hockey team in Toronto called the *Maple Leafs* and not the *Maple Leaves*? This is a question that has long puzzled hockey fans and commentators, though there is no record of any National Hockey League official or player puzzling over the nomenclature.

Steven Pinker, Montreal-born cognitive neuroscientist, asks the question in his probing study *The Language Instinct* (1994) in the context of the pluralization of word-formations. It seems our internal sense of grammar and word-formation distinguishes between nouns and nouns derived from names and treats them differently: "As for the Maple Leafs, the noun being pluralized is not *leaf*, the unit of foliage, but a noun based on the *name* Maple Leaf, Canada's national symbol. A name is not the same thing as a noun."

112. Whom do Canadians particularly despise?

So interesting would it be to draw up a list of the names of those men and women who are despised by Canadians that I decided to do so!

Here are the names, taken from the past and the present, that occurred to me. (I have refrained from including the names of controversial politicians who are both liked and loathed — people like Maurice Duplessis, Brian Mulroney, and Lucien Bouchard — whose legacies are mixed.)

François Bigot: Known as a corrupt intendant of New France, most historians consider him to be responsible for weakening the French forces under Comte de Montcalm.

Robert Stobo: An Italian officer with the French army, he acted as a turncoat and revealed to General Wolfe the location of Anse au Foulon, which Wolfe's men scaled, thereby taking the French troops by surprise on the Plains of Abraham.

Charles Lawrence: As lieutenant governor of Nova Scotia, he executed the orders of expulsion that removed Acadians from their traditional lands.

R.B. Bennett: Prime minister during the worst years of the Great Depression, Bennett offered no relief — and of equal importance no hope — to unemployed Canadians. He died on his estate in England, unloved and unrespected.

Adrien Arcand: He was the French-Canadian fascist and journalist who admired Mussolini and Hitler in the 1930s and 1940s.

Kurt Meyer: This Waffen-SS officer ordered the massacre of twenty-seven Canadian soldiers at Ardenne Abbey, Normandy ... they had already surrendered.

Clifford Olson: A serial killer. Olson confessed to murdering two children and nine youths in British Columbia.

Paul Bernardo: With his wife Karla Homolka, he was responsible for the deaths of the latter's younger sister and two teenage girls in St. Catharines, Ontario.

Robert Picton: This former pig farmer of Port Coquitlam, British Columbia, tortured and murdered a string of Native women over a period of years, burying their bodies on his farm.

Russell Williams: Colonel and officer commanding Canadian Forces Base Trenton, Ontario, Williams admitted to the murder of two women, to a series of assaults, and to innumerable burglaries.

113. Who was the first woman in Canada to be elected mayor of a city?

The temptation is to say that Charlotte Whitton was the first woman to be elected mayor of a Canadian city. That is true, for Ms. Whitton was the first woman to serve as mayor of the city of Ottawa. A former social worker, she served with distinction as a controller and then, upon the death of the incumbent in 1951, as mayor. The following year she was elected mayor, and in the process she bolstered equality for women across Canada.

Here's the trick: the key word isn't *first* or *woman* but *city*.

It is equally true that the first woman to be elected the mayor of any municipality in Canada was Barbara Hanley. On January 6, 1936, she was elected by the residents of Webbwood, a *town* some fifty miles west of Sudbury, Ontario. A schoolteacher by profession, Mrs. Hanley served for twelve years on the public school board and then one year on the town council. She retired as mayor after eight consecutive terms. Thereupon, she was appointed clerk-treasurer of Webbwood. She died in 1959 at the age of seventy-six, and was the first woman to be elected mayor in any municipality in Canada.

For this information I am indebted to Mrs. Grace LeBlanc of Guelph, Ontario, who felt that Mrs. Hanley should receive her due. And I agree.

114. Did Hitler visit Vimy Ridge?

Vimy Ridge, the site of a great Canadian and Allied victory and a turning point in the First World War, is marked with an impressive memorial that rises on the headland of the Douai Plane in Normandy. After the German occupation of northern France, the Adolf Hitler toured important and strategic sites, including Canada's monument at Vimy Ridge. For propaganda purposes, still photographs were taken of the leader and members of his entourage, all in uniform, as they posed beneath the soaring pylons of the Vimy Memorial. The event took place on June 2, 1940. The caption to the photograph, reproduced from an unnamed German-language newspaper in the files of the information centre at the Vimy Memorial, reads as follows (in an explanatory translation prepared for the present purpose by teacher Hans Knapp):

The Fuhrer at Vimy Ridge on June 2

In the background stands the Canadian World War I War Memorial which, according to an announcement by the British Minister of Lies, Duff Cooper, had been destroyed by the German barbarians. Our photograph is one of the most striking pieces of documentary evidence of the disgraceful lies disseminated by the British propaganda ministry. Meanwhile, in Canada's Parliament, the Canadian prime minister, Mackenzie King, has denied this accusation.

For many Canadians, it is a grim, triumphalistic image that conjures a period in European and North American history that will continue to haunt mankind for centuries to come. For other observers, it is proof that the Nazi dictator, who fought and suffered wounds in the First World War, appreciated the sufferings of soldiers on both battle lines.

115. How many times did Winston Churchill visit Canada?

Winston Churchill (1874–1965) was not only a world statesman, but also a world traveller, and he enjoyed nothing more than visiting cities throughout the British Empire, where he would orate before immense audiences on the benefits of British values and the virtues of the Imperial system. According to the British historian David Dilks, writing in *"The Great Dominion": Winston Churchill in Canada 1900–1954* (2005), Churchill visited Canada a total of nine times between 1900 and 1955, usually taking advantage its proximity to the United States for similar speaking engagements.

For more than a half-century, Churchill was an itinerant journalist and public figure, serving as member of Parliament, first lord of the Admiralty, chancellor of the Exchequer, and wartime prime minister of Great Britain during the critical years of the Second World War. Here are some notable visits:

- His first trip was a whirlwind tour to speak about Empire participation in the Boer War. "Thank God, we are once more on British soil," he exclaimed to the press, as he stepped off the Boston train at Montreal's Victoria Station.

- In 1929 he crossed the country in a private railway carriage.

- He made wartime visits in 1941 to Placentia Bay (off Newfoundland, not yet part of the Dominion) and in 1943 and 1944 to Quebec City.

- As Prime Minister he made visits in 1951 and 1955.

Dilks wrote, "Of no other Commonwealth country did Churchill have this lifelong knowledge, or anything resembling it." He professed admiration of Prime Minister Mackenzie King, but was worlds away from King's principle that "the great thing in politics is to avoid mistakes."

116. Who originated mobile document destruction?

Credit for originating the first mobile document shredding service goes to Greg Brophy, a Toronto businessman who founded Shred-it, a division of Securit Records Management of Oakville, Ontario. In 1987 it occurred to Brophy that a mobile shredding machine was the ideal answer to the need that businesses and corporations had for confidential document destruction, usually by shredding. That year he outfitted a van for this sole purpose. The next year Brophy established his company in Oakville to serve the Greater Metropolitan Area and soon mobile shredding vans parked outside corporations and businesses were a common sight in major cities around the world. Shred-it itself has grown to serve 150,000 customers through 130 branches on five continents.

117. How many prime ministers were Freemasons?

Six of our twenty-six prime ministers were Freemasons: Sir John A. Macdonald, Sir John C. Abbott, Sir Mackenzie Bowell, Robert Borden, R.B. Bennett, and John G. Diefenbaker. Is that a large number, or a small number?

A Freemason is a member of a semi-secret fraternal order, which is old if not ancient, practises secret rituals, champions a sense of brotherhood, and espouses philanthropy. It is estimated that some 200,000 Canadians are members of such orders — all of them men for the reason that women are denied membership. One early governor general is known for his Masonic affiliation: John George Lambton, 1st Earl of Durham. Since then, a good many lieutenant governors and provincial premiers have been Freemasons. From George Washington to Barack Obama, there have been forty-four U.S. presidents, fourteen of them Freemasons.

118. What do Hockey, Kingston, and Don Cherry have in common?

Kingston is considered by many sports historians to be the birthplace of ice hockey, Canada's national sport. In 1843 a British army officer stationed in Kingston recorded in his diary that he learned to skate and played hockey on ice here. Student clubs of Queen's University and the Royal Military College formed into an organized hockey league and played their games in the winter of 1886, using curved sticks and squarish pucks. So, Kingston is one of the original homes — if not the actual birthplace — of hockey and perhaps the birthplace of competitive hockey leagues.

What about Don Cherry? He was born in Kingston in 1934, and after being infected by the hockey bug, he played with the National Hockey League, coached for the American Hockey League, and became a celebrated but controversial — or celebrated because controversial — commentator on CBC-TV. Both his garb and his gab are colourful. He represents the spirit of "rock'em, sock'em hockey." The city of Kingston is a calm place, but nevertheless Kingstonites are proud of their city's hockey tradition.

119. Who is the architect Frank Goldberg?

The internationally famous architect Frank Gehry was born Ephraim Owen Goldberg in Toronto in 1929. He moved to California in 1947, and after graduating in architectural studies, he established his own practice in Los Angeles. In the 1950s, at his wife's instigation, he changed his last name to Gehry. Thereupon, he found his own highly individual style — post-structuralist and post-modernist; the buildings he designs seem to explode or implode, lurch or lean.

With the enthusiastic reception that followed the opening of his Guggenheim Museum in Bilboa in 1997, he claimed his rightful place in the constellation of "starchitects," famous and worthy of being considered in the same breath as Frank Lloyd Wright. When he was a youngster in his hometown of Toronto, Gehry visited the city's art gallery and was impressed with its Walker Court. He took pains to preserve it as something of a shrine when he was commissioned to oversee the renovation of the Art Gallery of Ontario. The renovated gallery was a phenomenal achievement, unveiled in December 2008.

120. Was a Canadian senator the oldest sitting politician in the world?

Yes. Senator Georges-Casimir Dessaulles (September 27, 1827, to April 19, 1930) holds the record as the oldest sitting politician, not only of Canada but also of the world. The Quebec businessman was a sitting member of the Senate of Canada when he died in 1930 at the age of 102. He was appointed to the Senate in 1907 at the age of eighty, so he served for twenty-three years. He had been president of the Bank of Saint-Hyacinthe and then mayor of the city.

It is said that he spoke twice in the Red Chamber: for the first time when he delivered his maiden speech, for the last time when responded to well-wishers on the occasion of his 100th birthday. This would not be possible today, for now the 105 appointed senators, or members of the Upper House, may serve from age thirty to age seventy-five.

121. Is Santa Claus a Canadian?

Santa Claus, in his red-and-white snowsuit with his bundle of toys "for good little boys and girls," must be one of the world's most-recognized figures and cherished symbols. Santa makes his home and workshop at the North Pole, so he is a figure of circumpolar interest.

He is considered to be a Canadian citizen. Indeed, in an official statement released on December 23, 2008, the minister of citizenship recognized his national status: "The Government of Canada wishes Santa the very best in his Christmas Eve duties and wants to let him know that, as a Canadian citizen, he has the automatic right to re-enter Canada once his trip around the world is complete."

Santa has a special place in the hearts of Canadians of all ages. For decades volunteers at Canada Post have been responding to letters addressed to him care of The North Pole, Canada, HOH OHO — they handled 1.2 million letters in 2007. The red and white of his snowsuit is also reminiscent of the Maple Leaf flag. As well, it is said that the NORAD installation at Alert, Nunavut, the world's most northern community, has been tracking the comings and goings of his sleigh and eight reindeer (nine with Rudolph) for the last half-century. In another sense he is a typical Canadian, being something of a do-gooder.

122. Has anyone ever served in both the House of Commons and the Senate without making a single speech?

Yes, that was the political achievement of Charles McDonald. "The Prince Albert pharmacist was elected to the House of Commons in 1925 but stepped aside a few weeks later so that defeated Liberal leader Mackenzie King could run in a safe seat. King never forgot the gesture and, upon returning to office in 1935, appointed McDonald to the Senate. But the pharmacist was too ill to take his seat." So wrote historian Bill Waiser, in "Letters to the Editor," *The Globe and Mail*, December 24, 2008. "McDonald is the only person in Canadian history to be elected to the House of Commons and appointed to the Senate who never uttered a word in either chamber."

123. Were any Canadian architects influenced by Frank Lloyd Wright?

Frank Lloyd Wright exerted a profound influence on architectural theory and practice, as well as on design and "organic" thought. His impact wasn't limited to the United States, where he introduced the so-called modern Prairie style as architect and teacher, but also in other countries, notably Japan, where he designed the landmark Imperial Hotel.

Wright had little direct impact on the Canadian architectural scene, he did influence active collaborator and disciple Francis C. Sullivan (1882–1929). Born in Kingston, Ontario, Sullivan practised in Ottawa and was Wright's sole Canadian pupil. He was studying with Wright at Taliesen in Phoenix, Arizona, when he died. Sullivan brought the modernist Prairie style to Ottawa, where he worked for the Canadian Department of Public Works from 1908 to 1911 and then conducted his private practice.

He designed the O'Connor Street Bridge in Ottawa, which was built in 1907; the Banff National Park Pavilion (a collaboration with Wright) at Banff, 1911; the Horticulture Building, Lansdowne Park, Ottawa, 1914; the flat-roofed Pembroke Public Library, Pembroke, Ontario, in 1913; as well as his own home, 364 Somerset Street, Sandy Hill, Ottawa, built in 1914. It is said that Sullivan supplemented Wright's trademark "horizontals" with a few "verticals" of his own.

Francis C. Sullivan is not the only Canadian architect whose work was marked by the influence of Wright. Another is James Strutt, who was influenced by Wright's smooth flowing lines. Strutt designed Ottawa's Macdonald-Cartier International Airport (now known as Uplands Airport), as well as the Saint Tekle Haimanot Ethiopian Orthodox Tewahedo Church (then known as St. Peter's Anglican Church), the Canadian Nurses Association headquarters, the Canadian Embassy in Algiers, as well as a great many private residences, including his own in Aylmer, Quebec. "That young man is going places," Wright is credited as saying about Strutt, early in the latter's career, according to Noreen Shanahan in "Ottawa Architect Championed Modernist Age in Canadian Design," the *Globe and Mail*, December 30, 2008.

124. Was Sir Frederick Banting's death an assassination?

Sir Frederick Banting was world-famous as the discoverer of Insulin and Canada's leading scientific researcher in the early years of the Second World War. It was said that his talents and connections were put to good use by the Department of National Defence. He also served as a liaison officer between the British and North American medical services. At the time of his death, he was engaged in top-secret, military-related research, believed to be in the area of biological weapons. He was killed on February 21, 1941, when the Hudson Bomber that was taking him to England crashed. The feeling has always been that the crash was no accident — that he was the target of an assassination.

William Roger Callahan, Newfoundland newspaperman, is the author of the fast-moving novel *The Banting Enigma: The Assassination of Sir Frederick Banting* (St. John's, Newfoundland: Flanker Press Ltd., 2005) which is a fictionalized account of Banting's tragic death. Was his death the result of a conspiracy to eliminate him? I conducted a brief correspondence with Mr. Callahan about the matter. On January 31, 2007, he noted, "There may well have been a conspiracy." He made the following six points:

1. Five identical aircraft, built in the same plant in California, are ferried together to Gander, Newfoundland.

2. The five take off together from Gander, in the space of about twenty minutes, bound for the U.K.

3. Four cross the North Atlantic as smoothly as a knife through butter, arriving at their destination in near-record time.

4. The fifth, Banting's plane, loses an engine some fifty miles out, turns back, then loses its second engine.

5. It crash-lands far off-course, and Banting and two of the three air crew perish. Only the pilot survives.

6. The Newfoundland government puts out a story about ice in the carburetors — but if one plane, why not all? Finally, the governor declared the inquiry report would not be made public (not in the public interest, he said). Similarly, the Banting autopsy report cannot be located.

These baldly stated facts make what might have been an accident based on equipment failure sound suspiciously like an act of sabotage.

The keyword is "suspiciously." No doubt for many decades questions will continue to be asked about the tragic death of this distinguished scientist and medical researcher.

125. Was Mandrake the Magician a Canadian?

Mandrake the Magician was the name and profession of the hero in the popular comic strip of the same name, which was created in 1934 by U.S. artist and writer Lee Falk (1911–1999). It is syndicated to newspapers by King Features to the present day. Artists who have contributed to the strip include Phil Davis and Fred Fredericks.

Mandrake conformed to the image of the stage magician of the 1930s and 1940s: a gentleman with slicked black hair, a pencil-line moustache, and who dressed in formal attire, sporting a scarlet-lined cape and a shiny top hat. The lovely Princess Narda and the husky Lothar were his assistants in his crusade against criminals and law-breakers. To this end he employed such magical powers as inducing hypnotic spells, creating illusions, and spreading the cloak of invisibility.

Lee Falk (who also created "The Phantom") maintained that Mandrake was his own creation, adding that in 1934 he had no knowledge of the stage appearances of Leon Mandrake (1911–1993), the Canadian-born magician and mentalist. Leon began his magic career in New Westminster, British Columbia, and he first toured with the Ralph Richards magic show. During the 1930s, he and his assistant/wife Narda performed their full-evening show throughout the United States. He appeared on stages and in clubs as a conjurer, illusionist, mentalist, manipulator, ventriloquist, and sometimes fire-eater. Later, he toured on campuses and in 1978 received a Performing Fellowship from the Academy of Magical Arts in Hollywood. His home base was in Surrey, British Columbia. Though he retired in 1985, his son Lon continues his work as a magician and showman.

Lee Falk said the similarity was coincidental. It "just so happened" that the title character in the comic strip "Mandrake the Magician" was named and drawn to resemble Leon Mandrake, right down to the pencil-line moustache, the formal attire, and so on. Even the names of the lovely assistants are the same. It does seem odd. Yet Leon did not mind the publicity attached to the popularity of the comic strip; in fact, he and Falk met in the 1950s and they corresponded. Presumably, each man regarded the double exposure as good for his business. Magicians are known to disappear from the stage, but rarely do they appear in two places at once — in the comics and on stage at matinees and evenings. In the strange and magical case of Leon Mandrake and Mandrake the Magician, they do double duty!

126. Did a French-Canadian inspire Sinclair Lewis's novel *Arrowsmith*?

The answer to this question is yes. In his day, Sinclair Lewis was the leading American author of a number of once widely read, controversial novels. Leading the pack is *Arrowsmith* (5), which earned him the Pulitzer Prize (which he declined), though five years later he accepted the Nobel Prize for Literature. His novel tells the story of Dr. Martin Arrowsmith, dedicated physician and innovative immunologist, and how he battled the establishment day in, day out. The character was modelled in part on Lewis's father, a family physician, but the main inspiration for the character and the conflict was the life, work, and personality of the French-Canadian immunologist Félix d'Herelle (1873–1941).

Born in Montreal, based in Paris, where he was briefly associated with the Pasteur Institute, and then with Yale University in Connecticut, d'Herelle was a talented microbiologist and the originator of Phage Therapy. In 1915 he established the use of antibacterial agents for therapeutic use, and he named these agents *bacteriophages* (or bacteria-eaters); he succeeded in isolating phages on September 3, 1917. Two years later he injected them into a patient to cure dysentery. His life and work are recalled in the naming of Avenue Félix d'Herelle in the 16th arrondissement of Paris.

Antibiotics like penicillin replaced virus technology for half a century, but antibiotic-resistant bacteria and the desire to return to the use of "natural" medications (like bacteria), the Phage Theory is reasserting itself. It would be pleasant to state that Canadian medical research contributed to the work of d'Herelle, but the truth is that until 2006, with Canadian breakthroughs in the treatment of cancer with viruses on the molecular level, not much was accomplished in his homeland, despite the role-model of Félix d'Herelle.

127. What is meant by the Sixth Family?

The so-called Sixth Family is a designation popularized by Lee Lamothe and Adrian Humphreys, crime reporters and authors of *The Sixth Family: The Collapse of the New York Mafia and the Rise of Vito Rizzuto* (2006). It refers to the Mafia crime syndicate headed by Mafia don Vito Rizzuto, based in New York from the 1980s to the early 2000s. Born in Sicily in 1946 and brought to Montreal as an eight-year-old, Rizzuto drew attention to himself as a "man of honour." He was inducted into the Bonanno Family. The so-called Five Families of New York are the Bonanno, Colombo, Genovese, Gambino/Profaci, and Lucchese families. It is popularly said that Rizzuto heads the Sixth Family. Rizzuto is called "the Canadian godfather" and "the John Gotti of Montreal." He has also been dubbed the "Teflon Don," because past criminal charges have had a tendency not to stick to him. It is sometimes said that the Sixth Family is larger than any of the other Five Families, due to the extent of the territory for which Rizzuto is responsible — all of Quebec and much of Ontario, including busy border crossings.

128. Did a Canadian ballerina appear in one of Charlie Chaplin's movies?

The answer is yes, and the movie is an interesting one. Charles Chaplin wrote, directed, and composed the music for his 1952 feature film *Limelight.* He also appeared in it as Calvero, a down-and-out music-hall performer who saves the life of a depressed and disheartened ballerina named Terry, played by newcomer Claire Bloom. There is a fairy-tale quality to the film as Calvero nurses Terry back to life and self-respect so that she may dance once again. Later, she assists him in his return to the stage. The "dance double" of Bloom, who was a fine actress but no dancer, was the prima ballerina Melissa Hayden, Toronto-born dancer and long-time featured performer with the New York City Ballet.

129. Who created the role of Old Lodge Skins?

Chief Dan George, chief of the Squamish, former British Columbia longshoreman, occasional performer, as well as Native spokesperson, played the part of Old Lodge Skins to perfection in the Hollywood movie *Little Big Man* (1970). On screen and off screen, principal actor Dustin Hoffman admired Chief Dan George and kept calling him "grandfather." George's inherent human dignity, verging on nobility of spirit, struck many chords in viewers. George was paid $9,000 (after taxes) for his role, according to John Eastman in *Retakes: Behind the Scenes of 500 Classic Movies* (1989). Eastman also noted that the role was first offered to three stars who declined it: Sir Laurence Olivier, Paul Scofield, and Richard Boone. Needless to say, their loss is the viewer's gain.

130. Did Fidel Castro ever visit Canada?

Fidel Castro, creator of modern Cuba and the man who wrested the Caribbean island from American capitalists and the influence of the American Mafia, made three visits to Canada.

The first visit was made after coming to power in 1959. He visited Montreal, and Prime Minister John G. Diefenbaker refused to meet with him. In 1995 he had an unofficial, four-hour stopover at the Vancouver International Airport, en route to Europe. On October 2–3, 2000, he was one of the world figures who attended the funeral of Pierre Elliott Trudeau, who was his personal friend.

131. Was a Canadian the inspiration for Dr. Moriarty?

The archetype of the "criminal genius" intent on subversion of the world order is Dr. James Moriarty, the astronomer and mathematician created by Sir Arthur Conan Doyle. Dr. Moriarty matches wits with Sherlock Holmes, Doyle's "great detective." The two men, each intent on the destruction of the other, lock in mortal embrace and plunge to their deaths at Reichenbach Falls in Switzerland.

Scholars agree that Doyle based Sherlock Holmes and his scientific method of observation and deduction on the *modus operandi* of his former instructor at the University of Edinburgh — Dr. James Bell. Did he do the same for Moriarty, and if so, who are the candidates? For the answers to these questions, I turned to the article "Sherlock Holmes and Some Astronomical Connections," contributed by Bradley E. Schaefer to the *Journal of the British Astronomical Association*, February 1993. Schaefer scours the Sherlock canon for the bad doctor's biographical details and professional credentials, noting that Moriarty is an astronomer and a mathematician. Schaefer quibbles with some of Doyle's scientific details, such as stating that Moriarty is "the celebrated author of *The Dynamics of an Asteroid* — a book which ascends to such rarified heights of pure mathematics that it is said that there is no man in the scientific press capable of criticizing it." Among Schaefer's informed criticisms is that the title would have been fine in the 1860s, but because of scientific advances by the 1880s, such a study would have been called *The Dynamics of Asteroids*.

Schaefer's view is that the likely inspiration for the mathematician and astronomer is the actual mathematician and astronomer Simon Newcomb. Newcomb's most famous paper is on the dynamics of an asteroid, and he was the world's most-honoured astronomer in the nineteenth century. Schaefer quotes a description of Newcomb's personality as being "dynamic and intimidating." He was "highly successful as a leader, in the sense that he got things done, but he was more feared than liked."

Newcomb was a force to be reckoned with, both as a scientist and a spokesperson for the scientific method, rather like the astronomer

Carl Sagan. He was a Canadian, or at least a Maritimer, in the sense that he first saw the light of day in Wallace, Nova Scotia, in 1839. He spent the rest of his life in the Eastern United States, where he held many important positions and received most of the scientific awards of his time. He died in 1909, late enough to read the early Holmes adventures. If he was familiar with the great detective (and who wasn't?) he may well have wondered about the correlation between his achievements and those of Dr. Moriarty.

So if Schaefer is right, Doyle modelled Dr. Moriarty on Professor Newcomb, the most famous Canadian-born scientist of the late nineteenth century.

132. Who was Canadian-born, Baskin or Robbins?

The popular Baskin-Robbins ice-cream outlets are found in cities throughout North America. The chain itself was founded with a single outlet in 1945 in Glendale, California, by Irvine Robbins, born in Winnipeg but raised from an early age in Tacoma, Washington. The entrepreneur convinced his brother-in-law Burton Baskin to join him in expanding the operation through franchise. Baskin-Robbins proved to be immensely successful for many reasons, one of them being the thirty-one ice-cream flavours (one for each day of the longest months of the year). They developed, produced, and dispensed hundreds of different flavours over the decades. Robbins was quoted as saying, "I never met a flavour I didn't like."

133. What is or was the so-called Indian Group of Seven?

Seven Native Canadian artists banded together in Winnipeg in November 1973 to exhibit and market their own artwork, as well as the paintings and sculptures of their colleagues. The fact that there were seven artists and that they were determinedly Canadian — like the original Group of Seven in the 1920s — led commentators to dub them the "Indian Group of Seven." Their joint exhibitions and marketing operations lasted until 1975, when the group disbanded. By then they had established their main point: that their art should be considered in aesthetic rather than ethnographic terms.

The talented group consisted of Jackson Beardy, Alex Janvier, Eddy Cobiness, Norval Morrisseau, Daphne Odjig, Carl Ray, and Joseph Sanchez.

134. Has Broadway ever dimmed its lights for a Canadian theatrical personality?

It is a custom on Broadway and the West End for legitimate theatres to dim their marquees to mark the passing of an outstanding theatre personality. Exactly when playhouses in New York City and London introduced this custom is unknown, but both cities dimmed their lights for three minutes in 1960 to mark the passing of songwriter Oscar Hammerstein II. Automobile traffic in New York's Times Square came briefly to a halt.

The custom was honoured on July 11, 2007, to mark the death of Edwin Mirvish at the age of ninety-two. He was known in Toronto as the proprietor of the discount department store called "Honest Ed's," but also respected in the world of the stage as a theatre owner. He saved Toronto's Royal Alexandra Theatre from demolition and from scratch built the city's Princess of Wales Theatre. For ten years, with his son David, he owned and operated London's historic Old Vic repertory company and theatre.

To mark the passing of this genuinely popular and audacious producer, proprietor, and patron of dramatic and musical theatre, Broadway's forty theatres dimmed their marquee lights for one minute on the Wednesday evening of his death. He is the sole Canadian to be so honoured.

135. Who is the goalie depicted in *At the Crease*?

At the Crease, the painting of a masked hockey player tending goal, is quite moving. The goalkeeper looks like a gladiator of old, armed with a stick and protected by gloves, shin pads, and an eerie white mask. It was painted by the realist artist Ken Danby, and Andrew Wyeth once told the painter that he thought *At the Crease* was both "terrifying and exciting." I am quoting from Ryan K. Danby's letter "The Man behind the Mask," which appeared in the *National Post*, October 11, 2007. This was shortly following the painter's tragic death, and the appearance of the article "Mystery Solved: The Identity of the Goalie in Ken Danby's Iconic Painting Is Finally Revealed," in which Randy Boswell reveals that it was Wayne Gretzky's opinion that the model for the goalie was an actual goalie named Dennis Kemp, who did appear in a photo-shoot for the artist. The artist's son denies this identity and maintains that his father had no individual goalie in mind: "The fact is that the goaltender in *At the Crease* has no identity. My father maintained this since the day he finished the painting. Because the mask conceals his face, the goalie is whoever the audience wants it to be: Ken Dryden or Tony Esposito or even that guy who recorded the shut-out during last Friday's house league game." The painting is all the more real for depicting the goalkeeper rather than a particular goalie. Ken Danby, in the present writer's presence, argued that he had no single goalkeeper in mind and that he should remain anonymous like the Unknown Soldier.

136. Who was the original Sea-Wolf?

The Sea-Wolf is a powerful adventure novel by Jack London. Published to great acclaim in 1905, it is the portrait of an able but brutish "sea captain" named Wolf Larsen, who captains his own seal-hunting schooner named *Ghost*. The novel is told from the point of view of a young man taken aboard the schooner, who comes to see the darker side of human nature exemplified in the Captain. Wolf Larsen is based on a real-life sailor and sealer named Alex MacLean, who sailed the waters of the Pacific Northwest in his vessel *Sophia Sutherland*. Captain MacLean, born on Cape Breton Island, was self-taught, strong-willed, and hard-hitting, rather like Jack London. MacLean was something of a legend for his exploits and personality before London met him and depicted him as Wolf Larsen. MacLean died seven years after the appearance of the novel, doubly legendary.

137. Has a Canadian author ever been awarded the Nobel Prize for Literature?

No Canadian author has ever been awarded the Nobel Prize for Literature. That statement excludes the laureate Saul Bellow, born in Lachine, Quebec, who was a naturalized American at the time of his acceptance. Yet, five Canadian authors have been nominated for the distinction. It must be borne in mind that nominations are not that difficult to arrange; to be officially nominated, one needs to have his or her name put forward to the Swedish authorities by a "responsible person" like a politician, a professor, or a previous laureate. The five nominees of the past are Wilson MacDonald, Irving Layton, Igor Gouzenko, Josef Škvorecký, and George Faludy.

In brief:

- MacDonald was a versifier in the 1930s and 1940s with a popular following.

- Layton was an outstanding poet who regarded himself as a "genius," and some readers agreed with his assessment.

- Gouzenko's contribution was to write (or co-write) widely read anti-Communist novels. Škvorecký emigrated from his native Czechoslovakia and published his own and other previously suppressed fiction in Canada.

- Faludy was Hungary's leading poet; he became a Canadian citizen during a twenty-year sojourn in this country.

Quebec novelist Yves Thériault argued that he deserved the award, and many readers who felt that the award should have gone to Robertson Davies now feel that Alice Munro is Nobel material.

138. Did Napoleon have designs on Canada?

It seems the French emperor did, if you believe what Stephen Leacock wrote in his essay titled "Reflections on the North," which appeared in *The Beaver*, December 1936. Now, Leacock is best known as a humourist, so he is never averse to some leg-pulling; but in his own day, Leacock was respected as an economist and an historian of the Canadian past. Not all his tales were tall ones.

In this essay Leacock explained that, in common with other generals, Napoleon preferred to attack the enemy's lines from the rear rather than the front. Here is what he has to say about marshalling troops in the Rockies and on the Prairies to assail Ottawa and Montreal:

> Well, at any rate, Napoleon's plan was to organize the vast tribes of the Northwest — presumably the Crees and the Doukhobors and the Albertans — to overwhelm Ottawa and Montreal. His idea was correct in a way and came true later on, but it was premature. It was characteristic of Napoleon's profound ignorance of America to imagine the Northwest filled with likely looking Indians who could be recruited into Kellerman's dragoons and Milhaud's cuirassiers and descend (in four or five days) from the Rocky Mountains on Montreal with cries of "Vive l'Empereur!"
>
> So Napoleon set out to get information. All that could be found out in Paris (the year was about 1805) was that a man called Mackenzie had been right across the continent to the Pacific Ocean and had written a book about it, published in 1801, under the title *Voyages on the River St. Lawrence and Through the Continent of America to the Frozen and Pacific Oceans*

— which, for a Scotchman, was short and snappy. Napoleon ordered the book translated in French and printed. Only two or three copies were made, beautifully bound and embellished. There is no trace of any of them left except of the copy given to General Bernadotte, afterwards, by Napoleon's influence, made Crown Prince of Sweden, and great-grandfather to the present King. Napoleon wrote to Bernadotte about the scheme, and hence our knowledge of it. The information gathered showed its emptiness — at the time — but later on the notion of a descent from Alberta to take Ottawa in the rear has been worked out with success.

Needless to say, nothing became of Napoleon's notion of conscripting Indian warriors under the leadership of French generals to invade the country from the Prairies.

139. Who is chief Ompa-pa?

Most people identify the French cartoonists Albert Uderzo and René Goscinny with their famous character Astérix, the ever-popular warrior of Ancient Gaul who battles (and bests) the Romans. They forget that this duo's first comic creation was a North American Indian chief named Ompa-pa (or Oumpah-Pah in the original French). The series first appeared in the weekly *Journal de Tintin* in 1958, and the strips were first published in book form in 1961. The French series called *Oumpah-Pah le Peau-Rouge* lasted until 1962.

Ompa-pa is the chief of the Flatfeet tribe, and he has a friend, a French officer named Hubert de la Pât Feuilletée (or Hubert de Flaky Pastry) or Hubert Brussels Sprout in the English version. Ompa-pa is called "le Peau-Rouge" or "Red-Skin" and he calls his friend "Two-scalp," a reference to the latter's orange-coloured wig. The series was inspired by conditions in New France in the eighteenth century, but it is vaguely depicted in terms of the North America plains. As one observer wrote, "Ompa-pa is strong and quick, and loves to eat pemmican. He is an honest and trustworthy brave whose simple heroism is comparable to that of the more famous Astérix, Uderzo and Goscinny's later creation. Hubert Brussels Sprout, whom the Flatfeet initially held as a prisoner, subsequently served as a mediator between the Europeans and the Native Americans, and is also an ally against the tribe known as the Sockitoomee, the sworn enemies of the Flatfeet." In one famous sequence in the series, Brussels Sprout introduces Ompa-pa as his dear brother, only to have his commanding officer remark, "When madam the Marquise your mother hears about this ..." Ompa-pa was overshadowed in 1959 by the phenomenally successful comic-strip series *Astérix le Gaulois*, introduced by Uderzo and Gascinny. Perhaps it is time for Ompa-pa to return!

140. What can politicians learn from William Davis?

The management style of long-time Ontario premier William Davis was the despair of many an opposition member. A small-c conservative, Davis had a knack for using evasive clichés like "with great respect," "if I may be permitted to say," "if in a real sense I can say," and "in this jurisdiction." Apocryphally, he said, "Never ever do today what can be put off for three years."

No one now remembers whether he or his long-time aide Clare Westcott coined the phrase "bland pays," but it did pay for them. Davis was the special bane of opposition members like Donald C. MacDonald, who in *The Happy Warrior* (1998) quotes Westcott as saying, "Taking quick action was considered sinful. When he's asked, 'Do you have trouble making up your mind?' his answer is, 'Well, yes and no.'" As Westcott observed, it was an accomplishment leading a series of governments, some of them minority governments, for fourteen years (1971–1985) and still remaining an optimist.

141. Who lives longer, the American or the Canadian?

Despite the degree of affluence and advanced health-care procedures in the United States, Canadians live healthier and longer lives than do Americans. "Canadians live about 2.5 years longer than Americans, on average." This information comes from the article "Score One for Canada" from the University of California's *Berkeley Wellness Letter*, July 2010. "Depending on which list you consult, Canada ranks either 8th or 11th among countries by life expectancy, while the U.S. ranks 38th or 50th. And yet, per-capita health-care spending in the U.S. is nearly double that in Canada and far higher than in any other country."

The article continues, "Canadians also tend to be healthier and stay healthier longer (2.7 more years of "perfect health," on average) than Americans ... the researchers attribute this disparity to the lack of (or inadequate) access to health care and more poverty in the U.S."

In terms of mortality rates in people ages fifteen to fifty-nine in 187 countries, a study in *The Lancet* showed that the U.S. has been falling behind other countries in reducing death rates. In 2010, the U.S. dropped to forty-ninth for women and forty-fifth for men. "This puts it behind all of Western Europe as well as lower — countries like Chile, Costa Rica, and Albania. Canada ranks 18th for women and 11th for men." Within the U.S., life expectancy is six or seven years shorter in Mississippi and Alabama than in Hawaii and Minnesota.

The article concludes, "We can do better." Americans can do better when it comes to the universal delivery of health care services, and so can Canadians.

142. Was the theologian Henri Nouwen a Canadian?

Protestants and Catholics alike like find inspiration in the spiritual writings of Henri J.M. Nouwen, the Dutch-born Roman Catholic priest and preacher. He offered university students and readers of his books a mystical interpretation of Christianity, which found Christ's love in serving those men and women and children who are "broken" in body or spirit.

He taught Pastoral Theology at Yale Divinity School and then Harvard Divinity School. At the invitation of Jean Vanier, he spent nine months in Trosly-Breuil, France, at L'Arche, the community for the handicapped. That led to the invitation to visit L'Arche Daybreak, the residential community at Richmond Hill, Ontario. Daybreak was the second such community to be established (after Vanier's at Trosly-Breuil) and the second-largest of the hundred or so such communities in the world. He served as Daybreak's pastor from 1986 to his death in 1996.

Father Nouwen spent the last decade of his life in Canada ministering to the physically and mentally handicapped residents of L'Arche Daybreak. He was sixty-four when he died, on a trip back to his native Holland. His body was conveyed to Richmond Hill and then to the burial plot on non-denominational land adjoining the cemetery of the Sacred Heart Catholic Church at King City, Ontario.

Father Nouwen's last lesson may well be the one embodied in the following passage from *The Inner Voice of Love: A Journey through Anguish to Freedom* (1996), the last book on which he worked: "Your body needs to be held and to hold, to be touched and to touch. None of these needs is to be despised, denied, or repressed. But you have to keep searching for your body's deeper need, the need for genuine love."

143. What was the connection between Shackleton's British Antarctic Expedition and Stefansson's Canadian Arctic Expedition?

One man was a member of both expeditions.

Commander Ernest Shackleton led the British Antarctic Expedition of 1907–09. Popularly known as the Nimrod Expedition, after the name of his flagship, this expedition consisted of a voyage followed by a trek to the South Pole, which was never attained, though the members of the group recorded on October 19, 1908, that "farthest south" was established, as was the location of the South Magnetic

Pole. James Murray, a Glasgow-born biologist, was the lead scientist with the expedition. He was forty-one at the time.

Vilhjalmur Stefansson was appointed commander of the Canadian Arctic Expedition, but he lost the flagship *Karluk*, under the command of Captain Robert A. Bartlett, when it became trapped in ice northwest of Wrangel Island in the Arctic Ocean. One dozen men perished there on September 7, 1914, including James Murray.

Murray, in addition to being a scientist, was a veteran explorer. Not many men tried to "attain" both the North Pole and the South Pole, but James Murray was one of them.

144. Why are Canadians such good hockey players?

Is it true that Canadians are the best hockey players in the world? Maybe, maybe not, but our country does produce outstanding hockey players, both amateur and professional.

Malcolm Gladwell has a theory as to why Canadians excel at the sport. We have an "utterly arbitrary advantage," he writes in his book *Outliers: The Story of Success* (2008). "Parents their ten-year-old children to play the game. Kids born in the first months of the year have an advantage over kids born in the last months of the year. They are older, stronger, and more mature. That makes a difference. Parents and teachers as well as coaches favour slightly older and more mature children than the others. Maturity is confused with ability. So the slightly older children receive a boost that propels them in later life ahead."

Gladwell, born in England, was raised near Elmira, Ontario, and is a graduate of the University of Toronto. He is a New York based essayist who has argued that what it takes to succeed is work, long hours of work. It takes practice to excel. Indeed, he says it takes "a magic number" — 10,000 hours of practice.

places

145. What are the Seven Wonders of Canada?

The Canadian Broadcasting Corporation conducted a survey among its listeners to identify the so-called Seven Wonders of Canada. Behind this undertaking lies the age-old idea that it is possible construct meaningful lists, such as the Seven Wonders of the Ancient World or Modern World. If such lists are plausible, why shouldn't there be similar lists of the Seven Wonders of countries like Australia or Bulgaria or Canada ... or even of provinces like Ontario ... or even of cities like Toronto?

In 2007 the call for Canadian wonder nominations was issued to CBC listeners, and the producers of *Sounds like Canada* and *The National* received more than one million entries, with suggestions ranging from natural wonders to human inventions. The CBC's judges determined "the winners among the wonders." Here is their list of the Seven Wonders of Canada:

- The Canoe

- The Igloo

- Niagara Falls

- Old Quebec City

- Pier 21 (Halifax)

- Prairie Skies

- The Rockies

There is no gainsaying the utility of the canoe as a mode of transportation, the igloo as a form of lodging, or the beauty of the cataract and the prairies and the mountains, or the historicity of an old city and the port of immigration. So the list is sound enough, if rather routine. Every listener of the program or reader of this book will have his or her own favourites to add, though for every addition there has to be a subtraction if the magic number of seven is to be respected!

I have my own list but it exceeds the magic number.

Here is my listing of Canada's natural and unnatural wonders, though it exceeds the magic number, and again is in no special order:

- The High Arctic: North Pole, North Magnetic Pole, northern lights

- Tommy Douglas's Medicare

- Antigonish Co-operative Movement

- Lester B. Pearson's Policy of Peacekeeping

- Perimeter Institute of Theoretical Physics (Waterloo, Ontario)

- Haida Gwaii (Queen Charlotte Islands)

- Burgess Shale (British Columbia)

- Group of Seven

- Transnational cultural institutions (crown corporations like the National Film Board and the Canadian Broadcasting Corporation).

Oops, there are nine choices here! I am *not* sorry about that!

146. Where and when did the country's greatest fire break out?

The greatest conflagration in Canadian history was the Miramichi fire, which broke out on October 7, 1825. "This forest fire was the largest so far recorded in Canadian history, the largest on the entire Eastern seaboard, a fire that burned across 6,000 square miles of northeastern New Brunswick — about one-fifth of the province — and killed at least 160 people." So wrote the historian Alan MacEachern, in "The Great Fire of Miramichi," *National Post*, October 31, 2000. So great was the destruction that it gutted the town of Newcastle. It was reported that embers fell on Prince Edward Island across the water.

147. What is the basis of British Columbia's economy?

It is generally accepted that British Columbia's economy is primarily based on resource extraction, notably oil and gas and forest products. But that ignores the province's illicit trade and traffic in marijuana.

In July 2001, the province's Organized Crime Agency (OCA) estimated that the province has between 15,000 and 25,000 illegal marijuana-growing operations. Each employs six persons and annually produces a crop with a wholesale value of $4 billion. All but 5% of the growth is exported to the United States. Export sales of marijuana are estimated to be larger than the export sales of wood and oil and gas, which are, of course, legal. It is said that more people in British Columbia are employed growing marijuana than the logging, mining, and oil and gas industries combined.

148. What are some mnemonics for remembering places in Canada?

Mnemonics are verbal memory aids, often making use of the initial letters of words in a list of items, so chosen to form new words or phrases that aid recall.

Mnemonics peculiar to Canada are few and far between. Here are the few that have been collected (lest they be lost):

ALSAMA, the names of the three prairie provinces from West to East: Alberta, Saskatchewan, Manitoba.

HOMES, the names of the five Great Lakes in no special order: Lake Huron, Ontario, Michigan, Erie, Superior.

"Some Men Hate Eating Onions," the names of the Great Lakes from West to East: Superior, Michigan, Huron, Erie, Ontario.

"Nice Northern Place Nestled Quietly Over Many States Always Befriendly Neighbouring Yankees," the names of the ten provinces and two territories from East to West before Nunavut.

JEWS, the names of four parallel streets in downtown Montreal: Jeanne Mance, Esplanade, Waverly, St-Urbain.

"Sir Charles God Damn Roberts", the order of the middle initials of the man-of-letters, Sir Charles G.D. Roberts.

"No New Prince," the names of the three Maritime Provinces: Nova Scotia, New Brusnwick, Prince Edward Island.

COSMOT, the names of the five native groups that formed the Iroquois Confederacy (also called the Six Nations Confederacy): Cayuga, Oneida, Seneca, Mohawk, Onondaga, Tuscarora.

"Spring Forward / Fall Back," how to adjust clocks: one hour forward in the spring for Standard Time; one hour back again in the fall for Daylight Saving Time.

149. Which part of Canada is both the oldest and the youngest part?

In a very special sense, Newfoundland — today's province of Newfoundland and Labrador — is both oldest and youngest. The island of Newfoundland was England's first colony. It was so claimed by Sir Humphrey Gilbert on August 5, 1583, and hence became England's oldest colony. Almost four centuries later, as the Dominion of Newfoundland, it entered into Confederation and became Canada's tenth and youngest province. This occurred on March 31, 1949, under the leadership of Joey Smallwood, its first premier. Thus, Newfoundland, the oldest colony, became youngest province.

150. Did Newfoundland change its name?

The province of Newfoundland was formed in 1949 with the Great Island's entry into Confederation. It had earlier been known as an island, a colony, and a dominion. A constitutional amendment, approved by the House of Commons on October 30, 2001, changed its name to read "Newfoundland and Labrador" in recognition of the fact that the province consists of both the island of Newfoundland and part of the mainland long-known as Labrador.

151. What is the meaning of the name *Ottawa*?

It is widely believed that the name *Ottawa* is derived from the Algonkian word for "barter" or "trade." If true, this would be fitting, as politicians in the nation's capital are called upon to barter or trade when it comes to policy and power. However, according to Native elder Basil Johnston, a specialist in Ojibway — the language of the *Anishinaubaek* — writing in *The Manitous: The Spiritual World of the Ojibway* (1995), it is likely that *Ottawa* derives from *ottauwuhnshk*, which means a river reed used as matting, bedding, and partitions. So perhaps Ottawans are people who nap a lot!

152. What is the Sea to Sky Highway?

The Sea to Sky Highway is a scenic stretch of British Columbia's Highway 99. The highway connects West Vancouver's Horseshoe Bay with the resort area of Whistler, a distance of about one hundred kilometres. Traffic on the highway must contend with hairpin turns around the coastal mountains. Its two lines were widened to improve British Columbia's bid for the 2010 Winter Olympics.

153. Is Canada among the major fishing countries of the world?

In 1990 the five largest fishing countries were the following (in decreasing size of industry): Japan, Soviet Union, China, U.S., Peru. On that listing, Canada ranked sixteenth among the world's major fishing countries. The ranking remains much the same today.

154. What is the nickname of Ottawa's Confederation Square?

To begin with, Confederation Square, within a stone's throw of Parliament Hill in Ottawa, is misnamed. Because it has three sides, it is a *triangle* and not a square. Pedestrian and vehicular traffic converge here from such busy streets as Wellington, Elgin, Rideau, Sussex, Colonel By, Mackenzie, Sparks, and Queen. Hence, to pedestrians and motorists in Ottawa, it is regarded as "Confusion Square."

155. Which city has a Film Street?

Film Street — its official name — runs off the main street of Trenton, Ontario. It leads to a small building that, during the early years of the twentieth century, acted as Canada's premier film studio. The best-known film produced there was *Carry on Sergeant*. This war movie is a silent film, and was released on 1928 — the eve of the introduction of sound to film.

156. Is there a Canadian village near Tokyo?

Niji No Sato is the name of a theme park that features English, Canadian, and Japanese villages. The park is located near Shuzenji on the Izu Peninsula, not far from Tokyo. According to Martin Robinson, writing in the *Daily Yomiuri*, January 5, 1995, the Canadian village is the park's main attraction. It features wood-boarded buildings, three totem poles, Native teepees, and a Native fort. The village is twinned with the city of Nelson, British Columbia, and hence bears that name.

157. What happened at Willson House in Gatineau Park on April 30, 1987?

On April 30, 1987, there was an eleven-hour meeting of the eleven first ministers at Willson House. The large mansion, which is used by mandarins for meetings, overlooks Meech Lake in Gatineau Park in the National Capital Region. It was here that the Meech Lake Constitutional Accord was drafted.

158. What do the place names "Quebec" and "Detroit" have in common?

What these two place names have in common is their etymology. Both *Quebec* and *Detroit* are names derived from words used by Natives that mean "narrows" or "strait."

159. Why is Demarcation Point well named?

Demarcation Point, in the Yukon Territory, is the name chosen by the Geographic Names Board for the northern point of the boundary of the Yukon-Alaska border. The southern point of this boundary is Mount St. Elias. The boundary itself lies along latitude 141 degrees West.

160. What is "the road that walks"?

The Algonkian-speaking Indians of Eastern Canada, it is maintained, referred to the St. Lawrence River, which is highly navigable and hence a great boon for travel and trade, as well as fishing and drinking, as "the road that walks."

161. What are *Zecs* in Quebec?

Zecs are privately owned and operated natural reserves (parks or wildlife reserves) that are found throughout rural Quebec. They are distinct from publicly owned-and-operated natural reserves.

162. What is unusual about the island in Middle Island Provincial Park?

Middle Island Provincial Park, New Brunswick, has been developed around an island that is the exact size and shape of a lake a short distance away. According to *The Great New Brunswick Discovery Booklet* (1991), Indian legend has it that the island was mysteriously lifted from the mainland, creating the lake, and then dropped into the river.

163. Why is Dartmouth known as the City of Lakes?

Dartmouth, Nova Scotia, is known as the City of Lakes because there are two dozen lakes within the city's boundaries. This may well be a world record.

164. What do New York and North York have in common?

The city of New York, in New York State, and the city of North York, which is part of the Greater Toronto Area in Ontario, were both named after the Duke of York, the official title for the brother of the King of England.

165. How is Timiskaming spelled?

Lake Timiskaming, which straddles the Ontario-Quebec border, is known in Quebec as Lac Témiscamingue. There is also the District of Timiskaming, yet some residents spell it Temiskaming. There are four possible spellings for the place name, which is Algonkian for "place of deep, dry water," according to "You Asked Us," the *Toronto Star*, September 22, 1991.

166. What is the name of the city that lies due south of Detroit?

The city that lies due south of Detroit is the Ontario city of Windsor. It seems counterintuitive that Canadians who live here should look *north* to see an American city.

167. Who is General John Cabot Trail?

The Halifax humorist Dave Harley goes by the amusing name General John Cabot Trail. Tangled together there are the names of the famous explorer John Cabot as well as Cape Breton's picturesque Cabot Trail in New Brunswick.

168. Which province's abbreviation is also the surname of a famous architect?

P.E.I. was, for a century, the official abbreviation of the province of Prince Edward Island. The initials match the surname of I.M. Pei, the Chinese-born American architect who is famous for the modernist design of his large-scale developments. For instance, he designed Toronto's Canadian Imperial Bank of Commerce building. He is not credited with the design of any buildings on Prince Edward Island.

169. Where is the World Blueberry Capital?

The town of Mistassini in Northern Quebec calls itself the World Blueberry Capital. Every August, *Le Festival du Bleuet* is held here. Candy shops sell chocolate-dipped blueberries, a local specialty. They taste sweet and tart at the same time.

170. Where is the Village of Artisans?

The community of Saint-Jean-Port-Joli is known as the Village of Artisans. It is located on the south shore of the St. Lawrence River between Rivière-du-Loup and Lévi. The Quebec village is renowned for the work of its artists and craftspeople, sell their work in boutiques, studios, galleries, and museums. Every summer it hosts the International Sculpture Festival. A statue in the town square commemorates the manoir of *seigneur* and author Philippe Aubert de Gaspé.

171. Which body of water produces the best duck in the world?

"As Canadian lakes go, the body of water roughly ten miles in diameter in Brome County, in Quebec's Eastern Townships, is a modest pool. But Brome Lake has become one of the best known of all Canadian place names: it is to Canada what Aylesbury is to Britain and Long Island is to the U.S. — the home of a domestic duck known as a great delicacy." So wrote Susan Cartwright and Alan Edmonds in *The Prime Ministers' Cook Book* (1976). They go on to explain that the fame of the Brome Lake duckling derives from a pleasant-tasting bird and the promotion of the duck-breeding farm at the lake.

172. Where is there a church built in the shape of a shell?

The Church of Fatima has the shape of a shell. It is located outside the municipality of Fatima on Ile du Cap aux Meules, one of the Îles de la Madeleine in the Gulf of the St. Lawrence. A tourist guide for the islands describes it as "a beautiful example of modern religious architecture. The simplicity of its interior decor adds to the pleasant and comfortable atmosphere of this church."

173. What is the setting of the world's first werewolf film?

Transylvania is a reasonable answer, with a nod to the classic cinematic version of Bram Stoker's novel *Dracula* starring Bela Lugosi as the king of the vampires. Predating this is the movie shot in 1913 by the Canadian director Henry McCrae. He based it on the short story "The Werewolves," written by Henri Beaugrand, which was set in New France in 1706. It told of a brand of cannibalistic Iroquois who camped at the mouth of the Richelieu River, south of Montreal. The Indians not only drank the blood of their victims and ate their flesh, but turned into *loups-garous* (werewolves) during the process of their horrible feast. *The Werewolves* is a silent motion picture so rare that no prints of it are known to survive.

174. Where was baseball invented?

As every American fan of baseball knows, sportsman Abner Doubleday of Cooperstown, New York, invented baseball, the quintessential American game, in 1838. Yet there is a description by Adam Ford of a baseball game played on June 4, 1838, in Beachville, Ontario — a town located between Woodstock and Ingersoll. It "stands as the first record of a baseball game played in North America," according to

Yvonne Butorac, author of *Great Exits* (1995) and writer of the column "Original Ontario," the *Toronto Star*, June 3, 1995. The game was a match between the Beachville team and one from the townships of Zorra and North Oxford. The event, which predates Doubleday's "invention" by one year, is marked by a display in the Beachville District Museum.

175. What is the name of the largest of the Thousand Islands?

Wolfe Island, in the St. Lawrence River, not far from Kingston, is the largest of the islands in the archipelago known as the Thousand Islands. Wolfe Island measures twenty miles by seven miles and dwarfs the rest of the (roughly) thousand islands.

176. Is it Georgia Strait or Georgia Straight?

Georgia Strait is the name of the body of water that separates Vancouver Island and the British Columbia mainland. *Georgia Straight* is the name of the populist tabloid founded in Vancouver in the 1960s. The two spellings are frequently confused.

177. What is Canadian about Edinburgh Castle?

The esplanade of the great castle at Edinburgh, Scotland, is considered to be Canadian territory; the reason for this goes back to 1625. The Scottish baronets who received land grants in Nova Scotia were required to "visit their lands" to claim them. Since this was inconvenient, it was agreed that they would have to set foot on the castle esplanade and this met the requirement. The Eastern end of the esplanade has been adorned with a plaque since 1953. It was unveiled in the presence of the premier of Nova Scotia, himself of Scottish heritage. The source for this information is the *Britain Vacation Planner*, spring 1998.

178. Is the correct name Arthabaska or Athabaska?

Arthabaska and Athabaska are names derived from a Cree word that means either "place of the bulrushes and reeds" or "meeting place of many waters." Today the names refer to two different places.

Arthabaska is the name of a town in Quebec located between Quebec City and Sherbrooke. It was here that Sir Wilfrid Laurier, future prime minister, opened his law practice.

Athabasca is the name of a town in Alberta, as well as a lake, a river, a pass, a landing trail, and a university. The town, which lies northwest of Edmonton, was originally known as Athabasca Landing.

179. Which company once owned 10 percent of all office space in Manhattan?

The claim is convincingly made that, in its glory days, Olympia & York Developments Limited owned ten percent of all office space on the island of Manhattan, including much of New York's Battery Park City. Founded by the Reichmann family of Toronto, the company is also credited with building First Canadian Place and commencing construction of the Canary Wharf project in London, England. The 1970s were a good decade for Olympia & York, but the 1980s were disastrous, with the collapse of property values, the tightening of bank credit, and the bankruptcy of the company itself late in the decade. Some things are too big to sink; Olympia & York resurfaced in the 1990s with development projects in Mexico and elsewhere. But never again would O&Y be described as "New York's biggest landlord."

180. Where is North America's largest botanical garden?

Montreal boasts North America's largest botanical garden. It is located near the Olympic Stadium and encompasses 180 specially landscaped acres of land, displaying 26,000 varieties of plants.

181. Is Beaver House located in Canada?

Beaver House is located in England. It is the name of the stately building in Great Trinity Square, London, that once served as the headquarters of the Hudson's Bay Company, which was chartered on May 2, 1670. With the sale of the Bay to Canadian interests, the office was closed. But the building remains there, as does its name, to this day.

182. What is secret about the Empress Hotel in Moose Jaw?

It is said that during Prohibition, bootlegger Al Capone would elude the Chicago police and take refuge in the Empress Hotel in Moose Jaw, Saskatchewan. To effect quick getaways, he had escape tunnels leading to houses of refuge burrowed beneath the building. Indeed, passageways exist, but these were constructed for maintenance purposes, not for Capone's flights in the 1930s.

183. Where is there a statue to Leo Tolstoy?

No doubt, the great novelist Leo Tolstoy is honoured with statues in his native Russia, but he is also honoured with one in Castlegar, British Columbia. In July 1987 a statue designed by Y.L. Chernov of the Soviet Union was erected in Castlegar during a dedication ceremony, which was held in the presence of Tolstoy's great-grandsons and Doukhobor leader Peter V. Verigin. Tolstoy was instrumental in raising funds for the settlement of Doukhobors on the prairies of Western Canada.

184. What part of North America was exempt from Prohibition?

The province of Quebec was the sole jurisdiction north of the Rio Grande that was exempt from Prohibition. In Canada, legislation of March 1918 ended the importation, manufacture, and trade of intoxicating beverages. The United States followed suit in January 1920. Quebec marched to a different drummer, and throughout the Prohibition era, the province remained "wet," while its politicians winked as the demand for booze in dry regions was met by bootleggers.

Prohibition and the bootleg trade continued until the United States repealed the Volstead Act on December 5, 1933. The temperance crusade was counterproductive. Consumption of liquor actually increased, and organized crime flourished. It was during this period that Montreal acquired the contradictory reputation of being "wide open but honest." At least one distillery was established in Montreal that operated in full compliance with the law.

185. Where will you find the town of Paradise?

Look no farther than Newfoundland's Avalon Peninsula. There, near Conception Bay, you will find — if not paradise itself — then at least the town. Paradise is not as romantic as it might seem, for it is essentially a suburb of the capital city, St. John's.

186. Where in Canada was Leon Trotsky imprisoned?

Russian revolutionary Leon Trotsky was imprisoned in Amherst, Nova Scotia, during the early days of the Russian Revolution. Arrested by the British on a ship bound for Europe, he was taken to Melville Island and then moved to the prisoner-of-war camp in Amherst. As Jim Lotz noted in a letter to the editor, in the *Globe and Mail*, December 16, 1987: "Perhaps there should be a plaque on the Enheat plant in Amherst, the former POW camp. The Russian Revolution nearly ended here. Trotsky upset the officer commanding the camp, and a guard almost stuck his bayonet through the Russian revolutionary. Perhaps the place could be designated a 'non-historic site.'" In his memoirs, the Russian revolutionary stated that the POW camp was the worst prison in which he had ever been incarcerated!

187. Is there duplication of place names in Canada?

There is duplication. Places that share names include Souris (Prince Edward Island and Manitoba); Windsor (Newfoundland, Nova Scotia, New Brunswick, and Ontario); Woodstock (New Brunswick, Prince Edward Island, and Ontario); Abbotsford (Quebec and British Columbia); Cochrane (Alberta and Ontario); Chatham (Ontario and New Brunswick), and many others.

188. What Canadian place names are frequently misspelled?

The names of a number of Canadian places are sometimes confused, garbled, or otherwise misspelled. Here, in alphabetical order, appear some place names and their misspellings:

Edmundston, New Brunswick: often spelled "Edmonston"

Geraldton, Ontario: often spelled "Geralton"

Gaspé, Quebec: sometimes written as "Gaspe" Bay

St. Catharines, Ontario: often given as St. Catherine's (with an "e")

St. John's, Newfoundland: often confused with Saint John, New Brunswick

Sidney, British Columbia: often confused with Sydney, Nova Scotia

189. What are some of the oldest place names in today's Canada?

According to toponomists, specialists in place names, the oldest Canadian place name from documentary records appears to be Newfoundland. The oldest name of native origin, also from documentary records, may well be the Miramichi River. The oldest name of all may well be Yukon River; the earliest immigrants from Siberia encountered this river, and presumably gave it its name, though there is no proof whatsoever that its earliest name was some sound like "Yukon."

190. Whose names are most featured in Canadian place names?

It seems that more places and features were named after Queen Victoria than after any other person. The Canadian most honoured in this way is Sir Wilfrid Laurier. In their day, the queen and the prime minister were well loved by Canadians of both English and French extraction.

191. Could Prince Edward Island fit into the area occupied by Lake Ontario?

Thomas D'Arcy McGee once said that someone should take Prince Edward Island and drop it into Lake Ontario. What McGee, the future Father of Confederation, had in mind was the reluctance of Islanders to join Confederation.

The claim has merit: the area of the island is 2,185 square miles, and the lake covers 7,550 square miles. Therefore, three P.E.I.s could fit into Lake Ontario, with a little legroom left over.

192. Which three provincial capitals lie north of the 49th parallel?

The 49th parallel is often described as the dividing line between Canada and the United States. Yet, much of Canada lies south of the 49th parallel, including seven of the ten provincial capitals. The only three provincial capitals that lie north of the 49th parallel are Edmonton, Regina, and Winnipeg.

193. Why is Winnipeg sometimes called "windy-peg"?

Although Chicago has the reputation of being the Windy City, it is hard to better the harsh cold winds that blow across the intersection of Portage and Main in downtown Winnipeg. Hence, the Manitoba capital city is sometimes called "windy-peg."

In the past, pedestrians were known to be blown across the intersection, so there are now underground walkways for pedestrians to use. According to Irene Marushko in "Famed 'Windy-peg' Corner a Walk on the Wild Side," the *Toronto Star*, October 31, 1998, Winnipeg is also known for its summer mosquitoes. The texts of four tall tales about the wind were cast in bronze and mounted at the intersection for the 1999 Pan American Games. Perhaps the tallest of the tales is that the north wind has blown the intersection itself four feet to the south.

194. Which island is Canada's most populous island?

Everyone knows that the country's largest island is Baffin Island, but the island with the largest population is a stumper. It is Île de Montréal (Montreal Island), which has a population of some 2 million.

195. Where is the world's shortest international bridge?

The world's shortest international bridge is the Thousand Islands International Bridge, which spans the St. Lawrence River through the Thousand Islands, linking the province of Ontario and the state of New York. It was dedicated by Prime Minister W.L. Mackenzie King and U.S. president F.D. Roosevelt on August 18, 1938.

The bridge runs from Ivy Lea, between Brockville and Gananoque, to Collins Landing, just west of Alexandra Bay. Its total length is 2,588 feet, about two-thirds of a mile.

196. What is *Picture of Light*?

Picture of Light is the title of a feature documentary film about the northern lights. The 83-minute film, released by Grimthorpe Film in 1994, was written, produced, and directed by Peter Mettler. Accompanied by a meteorologist, the director travels to Churchill, Manitoba, where he observes, discusses, and photographs magnificent, curtain-like displays of the aurora borealis. They discuss the displays from perspectives that are magical, spiritual, and scientific. They also interview tourists who have travelled to the Arctic Circle from as far away as Japan to witness the spectacles of the northern lights (and to conceive children under the northern lights). The auroral displays are truly spectacular and awe-inspiring.

197. Which Great Lake's waters do not flow over Niagara Falls?

There are five Great Lakes and the waters of four of them cascade over Niagara Falls. The waters of Lakes Superior, Huron, Michigan, and Erie collect and flow into the Niagara River, which plunges over the falls at Niagara. Then they enter Lake Ontario before they join the St. Lawrence River and empty into the Atlantic Ocean. Hence, the waters of Lake Ontario do not take the plunge over Niagara Falls, as they have already done so.

198. Where are you guaranteed to see Ogopogo?

Ogopogo is a creature said to inhabit the calm waters of Lake Okanagan in the interior of British Columbia. Few, if any, of the tourists who visit the Okanagan Valley in the summer will report spotting the serpent-like creature. But most of the tourists will see effigies of Ogopogo in Kelowna and Vernon, cities located on the shores of the Lake.

In fact, Ogopogo has two likenesses in Kelona. One is a green statue with a forked red tongue that was erected at the intersection of Bernard Avenue and Abbot Street. The other image looks down from the totem pole carved by Oliver Jackson in 1955 to mark the city's fiftieth anniversary. In Vernon, Ogopogo takes the form of a green, serpentine fountain in Polson Park. Additionally, between Kelowna and Vernon, on the shoulder of Highway 97 that overlooks Lake Okanagan, there stands an official marker, erected by the Department of Recreation and Conservation, which identifies Squally Point as "Ogopogo's Home."

199. Is there a sasquatch memorial in Western Canada?

No, there is no memorial anywhere in Canada to the sasquatch, the enigmatic giant of the Northwest. However, a public park that lies north of Harrison Hot Springs in the interior of British Columbia, where the creature is said to have his haunt, is officially named Sasquatch Provincial Park. In the words of one travel writer, "The park's visitors are more likely to sight bald eagles, great blue herons, and mallards than they are to spot the legendary monster."

There are a number of memorials to the giant in the Western United States, where the sasquatch is known as Bigfoot. The biggest memorial is an eight-foot statue — sculpted in wood by Bigfoot enthusiast Jim McClarin — that stands at the junction of Highways 299 and 96 at Willow Creek, Northern California.

200. Does more snow fall on Canada than on any other country in the world?

Way back in 1986, I addressed a dozen students enrolled in the Media Arts Department of Sheridan College of Applied Arts and Technology. With the approval of their coordinator and for course credit, they undertook to research some subjects that had long interested me. One student was saddled with the question on comparative snowfall in Canada and Russia. He talked with science librarians, specialists at Environment Canada, and finally that body's climatologist David Phillips. Phillips stated authoritatively that a comparison of Canadian and Russian annual snowfall is impossible to ascertain or even estimate, as not only is the amount of snow over an area not recorded (rather, what is recorded is the number of inches/centimetres at one location), but the Russian authorities do not publish their meteorological statistics. So not every question has an answer. The larger the northern country, the larger the snowfalls — this formula would seem to make sense, and Russia would win the snowfall stakes as a bigger country than Canada, but there is no way to know for sure. I awarded the student top marks for persistence.

201. Where was ice hockey first played?

The origin of hockey — teams taking turns hitting a ball or puck with a stick toward goals on ice or a field — is as old as the hills. There are early Dutch paintings that show townsfolk enjoying themselves playing stick-ball games on fields as well as ice. But the modern game could be described as Canadian in origin, except for the fact that the competitive sport is older than the Dominion of Canada, which was formed in 1867.

Various British garrison cities claim the honour of being "the birthplace of ice hockey": Kingston, Ontario, in 1843; Windsor, Nova Scotia, in 1844; Montreal, Quebec, in 1875. The basic rules and regulations were established with a match at Montreal's Victoria Skating Rink, Marc 3, 1875. But perhaps pride of place should go to the settlement of Fort Franklin (renamed Deline in 1933), Northwest Territories.

There exists a long-unread letter, found by historian Joseph Nieforth and discussed by journalist Randy Boswell in "Franklin Missive Mentions Hockey," the *Ottawa Citizen*, May 3, 2003. This letter was written by the Arctic explorer Sir John Franklin in November 1825 and addressed to the British geologist Roderick Murchison — it also mentions the words "ice" and "hockey" in the same sentence. It was penned from the winter quarters of Franklin's Second Arctic Expedition, on the site now known as Deline, which is along the shore of frozen Great Bear Lake. The key passage runs as follows: "We endeavour to keep ourselves in good humour, health and spirits by an agreeable variety of useful occupation and amusement. Till the snow fell, the game of hockey played on ice was the morning's sport. They were invariably joined by the officers. By thus participating in their amusements, the men became more attached to us, at the same time that we contributed to their health and cheerfulness."

202. Where is North America's oldest annual sporting event held?

North America's oldest annual sporting event is held in St. John's, Newfoundland. The inaugural race of the St. John's Regatta was held in the city's harbour on September 22, 1818, to celebrate the 58th anniversary of the coronation of King George VIII. A decade later, the contest moved to Quidi Vidi Lake, in the city's east end, where it has been held annually since then. The racing event draws 400 competitors — two-thirds of them female. (John DeMont, "Homage to Tradition," *Maclean's*, August 4, 2003.)

203. Why is West Point grey in colour?

This question is asked by Hans and Allyson Tammemgi in *Exploring Niagara: The Complete Guide to Niagara Falls and Vicinity* (1997). They are referring to the U.S. military academy known as West Point. Apparently, the colour of the uniforms of West Point cadets has been grey since the War of 1812, when American forces defeated the British in the Battle of Chippawa in 1914. "Due to a shortage of supplies, none of the regular blue uniforms were available and the army had to march to battle wearing grey instead. Legend has it that in honour of this victory, West Point cadets today wear grey."

204. Does Toronto's city hall appear in a *Star Trek* episode?

Indeed, it does. The episode titled "Contagion," part of *Star Trek: The Next Generation*, telecast March 20, 1989, shows Captain Picard and Data standing before an Iconian gateway. This is a portal that allows them to travel to various points in the galaxy. "Various locales appear, including the bridge of the *Enterprise* and the unmistakable fountains of Nathan Phillips Square and the uniquely curved towers of Toronto

City Hall." This information comes from "Cityscape," *Toronto Post City Magazine*, December 2003.

205. Where will you find over one thousand clocks?

There are more than a thousand Canadian-made and Canadian-label clocks, as well as other timekeeping devices, in the collections of the Canadian Clock Museum in Deep River, Ontario.

This unique museum was founded in December 1999 by Allan Symons, a local clock collector, as a non-profit organization. The museum, which opened to the public in May 2000, is dedicated to preserving and promoting the history of Canada's clocks. It is the country's sole clock museum. This is a surprise when one considers the singular importance of timekeeping in a country with many time zones, the National Research Council Time Signal, and the country's global contribution to Standard Time.

On display are hundreds of Canadian-made mantel, wall, grandfather, alarm, and advertising clocks that date from the early 1800s to present, as well as hundreds of horological documents and publications. Visitors to the museum receive a personal guided tour and are able to tell the time of day using clocks like the Canadian Neon-Ray, Arthur Pequegnat, Westclox, Snider, Ingraham Canadian, Breslin Industries, Canadian General Electric, and Blackforest. There are several unique examples, including a grandmother clock that came from the Midgets Palace in Montreal. Should a timepiece go wrong, the museum has a solution — it boasts a resident conservator who is also a clockmaker (the term for someone who restores clocks).

The museum's appealing, informative website offers a virtual tour. Curiously, when I accessed it on January 1, 2004, I found that it lacked a timepiece of its own! It seems that the problem has since been remedied, though.

206. Where is the Potato Museum located?

The world's sole museum devoted to the humble potato is the Prince Edward Island Potato Museum. It is located in the town of O'Leary on the western part of the island.

Opened in 1993 and expanded in 1999, it opens its doors every summer to visitors and potato-lovers from mid-May to mid-October. Members of the public are greeted by the Giant Potato, a fibreglass effigy of an upright potato that rises 14 feet in height and expands 7 feet in diameter.

Visitors walk through the Potato History Exhibit, the Machinery Gallery, the Potato Hall of Fame, the Amazing Potato Exhibit, the Community Museum, the Resource Room (with gift shop), and the Heritage Lane, which offers the Heritage Chapel, Log Barn, and Log Railway Station. To be added are the Fire Hall and Telephone Office. During the last week in July, the Potato Blossom Festival is held.

"Bud the Spud" (a phrase coined by Stompin' Tom Connors) never had it so good! The common potato is an important export of Prince Edward Island. But considering the importance of this vegetable to the health and well-being of mankind, perhaps it is worthy of even greater general interest and appreciation.

207. What feature of the Canadian skies was described by Galileo?

The Italian mathematician, astronomer, and physicist Galileo Galilei was the first person to use the telescope to study the heavenly bodies. Around 1610 he observed and described the luminous phenomena visible in the upper atmosphere that occurs in the high latitudes of both hemispheres. It is sometimes said that Galileo named the display in the northern hemisphere the *aurora borealis* or northern lights, in the southern hemisphere the *aurora australis* or southern lights. This is not known for sure, as naming these curtain-like displays of shapes and colours in the night skies is also credited to the French scientist, mathematician, and philosopher Pierre Gassendi in 1621.

208. What is remarkable about the waters of Lac Ste. Anne?

The waters of Lac Ste. Anne, a small lake some seventy kilometres west of Edmonton, are said to have powers that are healing, recuperative, restorative, and spiritually revitalizing. To the native Cree, it was known as Manito Sakahigan (Lake of the Spirit). In 1844, missionary priest Jean-Baptiste Thibault gave the lake its present name in honour of the mother of the Virgin Mary, and it became a pilgrimage site as early as 1889. Each year there is a gathering in July that attracts pilgrims who wade and swim in its waters. It is the largest gathering of its kind in North America and is attended by pilgrims from around the world.

Belief in the power of water to heal is common to all world religions, and the notion of "healing waters" is a standard folklore motif. Yet, there is something special about Lake Ste. Anne. Source: "Waters for the Spirit," *Maclean's*, September 6, 2004.

209. Where did Babe Ruth hit his first professional homer?

As unlikely as it might seem, baseball legend Babe Ruth hit his first professional home run — a three-run shot — from Hanlan's Point Stadium, a long-gone ballpark on Toronto Island. This took place during an International League game played on September 5, 1914, and the ball landed with a splash in Lake Ontario. Ruth was playing with the Providence Grays against the Maple Leafs. He went on to become a major-leaguer, first with the Boston Red Sox and then with the New York Yankees.

A municipal plaque marks the site on Toronto Island, but Jerry Amernic, author of the delightful novel *Gift of the Bambino*, which was inspired by the incident, has long pushed for provincial recognition of the site. The Toronto Blue Jays backed the scheme.

Rumours have circulated for three quarters of a century that Babe's ball was retrieved and kept by a Torontonian as a souvenir, as noted by Randy Boswell in "Heavy Hitters Want Toronto Shrine to Babe,"

National Post, November 25, 2004. While that is unlikely, there are baseball enthusiasts who would like to see Lake Ontario drained to uncover the ball! Amernic is more modest in requesting provincial recognition of the site. "Babe Ruth was a monumental figure whose impact exceeded that of any athlete. The place where he hit his first pro home run is special."

210. Who is Loyalist Man?

Loyalist Man is a familiar sight to residents of Saint John and to tourists who drive the highway that leads to the Reversing Falls, one of New Brunswick's tourist sites. *Loyalist Man* has stood by the side of the road, welcoming people to the falls since the 1960s. In a way he is as memorable as the falls themselves.

"The painted plywood United Empire Loyalist, seven metres tall with a tricorn hat, blue frock coat, stockings and gay grin, looms like an eighteenth century superhero and has long served as a tourism logo for the port city," wrote Shawna Richer in her article "Thoughts of Banishing Loyalist Man Stir up Emotions in Saint John," the *Globe and Mail*, December 3, 2004.

The wood cut-out symbolizes Loyalist heritage. Some ten thousand Loyalists arrived from the United States in 1783, and the next year Saint John became the first incorporated city in today's Canada. But the past is passé to developers of the city's Harbour Passage waterfront project who wish to remove Loyalist Man and replace him with a fountain and park. Nobody seems to know where he could go. Heritage groups and the general public want *Loyalist Man* to stay put.

211. What day did the population of Gander, Newfoundland double?

At the time of the last census, the population of Gander, Newfoundland, was 10,339. Located in a fog-free area of east-central Newfoundland, it serves as a refuel stop for transatlantic flights. The population doubled on September 11, 2001, following news of the terrorist attacks in New York, Washington, and rural Pennsylvania. All airports in the United States were closed to international flights and flights underway were grounded or rerouted.

Fifty-three international flights landed at Gander alone. The Red Cross reported that they had to process 10,500 passengers from all the airplanes. Despite the fact that there were only 550 hotel rooms in Gander, this was accomplished in an orderly fashion, with "the Plane people" being hosted by townsfolk of Gander and nearby communities, or being housed in high schools and other public buildings. To fill in the time of the unscheduled stopover, which in some cases lasted two nights and three days, passengers were provided with excursions including boat cruises. Many friendships were formed between grateful American passengers and local people. So Gander's population swelled to 20,889 for twenty-four or more hours.

The figures here are estimates, and estimates vary. Another account lists thirty-nine diverted flights and 6,579 marooned passengers and crew members. If those figures are correct, Gander's population did not double, but it rose by two-thirds.

Gander was one of a number of Canadian cities affected by emergency precautions occasioned by the 9/11 terrorist attacks. A total of 240 flights were rerouted from the United States to Canada. Four years later, U.S. president George W. Bush expressed the gratitude of the U.S. Government by making a speech at Pier 21 in Halifax. Individual Americans, whose lives were affected and even enriched by the tragedy, raised funds for scholarships to aid Newfoundland students of the Gander area.

212. Where is Pier 21?

Pier 21 is the port on the Halifax waterfront that received immigrants and refugees arriving by ship. Between 1928, when it was opened, and 1971, when it was closed, Pier 21 received one million newcomers. During the Second World War, a half-million servicemen and women left for overseas from Pier 21, so it has in its way as many memories as New York's Ellis Island. It is now a National Historic Site; since 1999 it has served as a museum. The Rudolph P. Bratty Exhibition Hall offers visitors mementoes of the nearly fifty years that Pier 21 allayed fears and encouraged hope in new immigrants. Over the years it has attracted millions of tourists and visitors — many more people than it ever received in immigrants.

213. Is Montreal the world's second-largest French-speaking city?

It used to be popular to claim that Montreal was the world's second-largest French-speaking city. (Naturally, pride of place went to Paris, as befitting the more-populous capital of France.) However, during the so-called Quiet Revolution of Quebec in the 1960s, followed by the passage of French-first, English-second "language laws" in its wake, the claim that Montreal came second to anything went unasserted even in tourist promotion. After all, it was the aim of the Parti Québécois to assert, whenever possible, that the French language was everywhere endangered, particularly in Quebec. However, Mark Abley, the author of *Spoken Here* (2003), a study of the status of the world's languages, suggests that the silver medal should be awarded to Kinshasa, the much-more-populous capital of the African country Zaire. However, now that Zaire has replaced French with English as the country's official second language, it is possible that in the future, Montreal — with bronze status today — will again claim the silver medal.

214. Where in Canada are you always in Love?

Tricky question.

Love happens to be the name of a village on the CP Rail line northeast of Saskatchewan. It is believed that no other place is so named in

North America. As for the name itself, the popular view is that it was named such after young lovers were found on a siding of the newly laid railway tracks, but it is more likely the site was so named after the CP conductor Tom Love, who dubbed it Love Siding when he passed through in 1930. It became the Village of Love in 1945.

On Valentine's Day 1993, the postmaster first made use of the postmark, adorning it with the image of a seated teddy bear holding a giant heart, circled by the words "Canada Post — Postes Canada — Love, Saskatchewan." Since then, the postmark has been prized by people from around the world, who mail letters to the postmaster in Love and request that the enclosed envelopes be stamped and franked with the desired postmark. On Valentine's Day, the mail is particularly heavy!

In 2005 the population of Love, Saskatchewan, was listed as fifty-one inhabitants, as noted by Darren Bernhardt in "51 People Who Are Always Truly in Love," *National Post*, February 12, 2005.

215. What territory became part of Canada on April 1, 1999?

Nunavut became part of Canada on that date, which was coincidentally April Fool's Day! It covers 1.9 million square kilometres of the eastern Arctic. It was formed from the eastern part of the Northwest Territories.

216. What is the significance of Mile 3,339?

There is a simple white marker in a farmer's field in Shuniah Township, northeast of Thunder Bay, Ontario. It was erected by the Ontario Ministry of Transport but it is privately maintained. It marks the point on the Trans-Canada Highway at which the one-legged marathon runner Terry Fox collapsed. To raise funds for cancer research, he covered 5,374 painful kilometres, more than half the distance from

Halifax to his home in Burnaby, British Columbia. The official point of commemoration is the Terry Fox Scenic Outlook, some miles farther west. The sign reads: "Mile 3,339 / Terry Fox's / 'Marathon of Hope' / September 1, 1980."

217. Where does a soldier shed a tear?

There is a tear that runs down the right cheek of one of the five soldiers depicted in *Remembrance and Renewal,* the giant sculpture that is the centrepiece of the Juno Beach Memorial, overlooking the English channel in northeastern France. In the ring formed by the helmeted soldiers, the tear appears on the cheek of the warrior who faces where the coast of Normandy was stormed by 21,000 Canadian soldiers on D-Day ,1944. Some 2,000 Canadians died in the assault, which freed France and then Europe from the grip of German occupation. Dedicated to all Canadians who served in the Second World War, the memorial depicts, in a semi-abstract manner, five soldiers who rise as if from a burst of shrapnel and hover protectively over the viewer.

The powerful black sculpture with its brooding-yet-defiant figures was designed and cast in bronze by the sculptor Colin Gibson of Priceville, Ontario. It forms part of the Juno Beach Centre, near Courseulles-sur-Mer, which was officially opened on June 6, 2003. Both the sculpture and the centre itself (designed by Toronto architect Brian Chamberlain) are based on five points or orientations, which are meant to symbolize the five points of the Maple Leaf.

The centre offers visitors to the battlefield permanent and rotating exhibits, but its centre point remains *Remembrance and Renewal.* At the time of commission and installation, there was much debate about the inclusion of the teardrop; some members of the professional officer corps felt it was inappropriate to display private sentiment in the context of recognition of a public act of service and sacrifice. But the display of emotion was immediately popular with the group of veterans who formed a voluntary association to commission and finance the sculpture and Juno Beach Centre. It has remained popular and been judged appropriate by its thousands of visitors each year.

218. What is the largest community north of the Arctic Circle?

Inuvik is the largest Canadian community north of the Arctic Circle. It lies at 68 degrees 21 minutes longitude and 133 degrees 43 minutes latitude. Its year-round population in 1998 was 3,296.

219. What is *le Circuit des Filles de Caleb*?

Le Circuit des Filles de Caleb is a tour of those sites in the village of Saint-Stanislas, near Trois-Rivière, that are associated with the Pronovost and Bordeleau families featured in the novel *Les Filles de Caleb* (1985). Immensely popular in Quebec, the novel was written by Arlette Cousture and became the basis of the equally popular *téléroman* or television mini-series. The tour begins at Musée des Filles de Caleb.

The novel was translated by Käthe Roth as *Emilie: A Novel* (1992), and the Quebec *téléroman* was re-released in an English-dubbed version as *Emilie*. Perhaps the most grandiose tribute is *Village d'Emilie des "Filles de Caleb"* — a theme park that doubles as the outdoor and indoor sets used in the making of such popular-in-Quebec television series as *Les Filles de Caleb*, *Shehaweh*, and *Blanche*.

220. What lies between Gold and Sword?

The answer is Juno. Gold Beach and Sword Beach flank Juno Beach, the sector of the Allied landing coast of Normandy assigned to the Canadian forces. British Infantry divisions stormed Gold and Sword; Canadian infantry divisions took Juno. These divisions consisted of ten battalions of Canadian infantry, supported by three armoured regiments.

Juno was the code name of the amphibious assault on this stretch of the northern coast of Nazi-occupied France — an important part of Operation Overlord and the turning point of the Second World War. It is often described as "the longest day." Ted Barris's *Juno: Canadians at D-Day, June 6, 1944* (2004) is a fine account of the Canadian participation in Operation Overlord.

About Juno, Barris wrote: "One amusing story about the coding origins for the Normandy landing sites suggests that SHAEF contemplated naming the British and Canadian beaches after fish; that is, Gold Beach as in goldfish, Sword Beach as in swordfish, and Jelly as in jellyfish. A Canadian, the story continues, informed the British that jelly had a much different and less attractive connotation in North America. Consequently they chose Juno instead."

Some 20,000 Canadians participated in the assault on the Juno section of Hitler's "Atlantic Wall." The dead and badly wounded numbered 960. The total invasion force was close to 200,000 men against an estimated 175,000 German troops, who had the benefit of positions that had been entrenched for years. Hitler's vaulted "wall" was breached within hours. The next morning, D+1, it was apparent that the invading Canadian forces had taken and held more ground than the other Allied forces.

As Ted Barris noted, "Within forty-eight hours of D-Day, people in Britain saw Sgt. Bill Grant's film sequences, including the first images of the Allied troops, the Queen's Own Rifles of Canada, landing in Normandy. Even before that, the raw footage was flown across the Atlantic and shown to North American audiences." This was a remarkable achievement, and would be even today, with access to videography and the internet.

221. British Columbia is the major source of which ornamental stone?

British Columbia is a major source of jade. It shares the market with the world's other leading producer, Siberia. A highly valued mineral-like substance, Jade is found in small quantities the Yukon, the Northwest

Territories, and Newfoundland, but its heaviest concentrations are in northern British Columbia.

Jade is not technically a mineral, but rather a hard, mineral-like substance, generally dark green in colour, commonly used as gemstones or in sculptures that are identified with Chinese craftsmanship. In fact, Canadian jade is quarried or mined in British Columbia, shipped to China, worked into artistic shapes, and then shipped to world markets which include British Columbia!

Jade is an aggregate or a blend of minerals, and there are two types based on their chemical and mineral compositions. These are called nephrite and jadeite. The former is the type found in Canada. Jadeite, which is encountered in Burma, Central America, and China, is considered more desirable, and hence more valuable. Interestingly, what is called "Polar Jade," found in British Columbia's Dease Lake area, is most highly prized, despite being nephrite.

As Stan Leaming writes in *Jade Fever: Hunting the Stone of Heaven* (Surrey, British Columbia: Heritage House, 2005), "Jade is a depleting asset like all mineral commodities, but the relatively small demand and large reserves are likely to be maintained for some time to come, and the small but vital industry should continue into the distant future."

222. Is the Chilkoot Trail in Yukon Territory?

The Chilkoot Trail is identified with the Klondike Gold Strike, which took place in Yukon Territory of the Canadian North. The steep mountain pass led prospectors to the Klondike goldfields in 1897, so it is commonly assumed that the trail is a pass through the territory, but truth to tell, the trail lies south of the Yukon. Approximately one-third of the trail lies in Alaska and two-thirds in northern British Columbia. Prospectors landed by ship on the Alaskan coast, climbed the trail (often many times with their backpacks), and then proceed to the gold-rush fields to seek their fortunes. Many of them found wealth after climbing the Chilkoot Trail.

223. How many Canadians live south of the 49th parallel?

When asked, most Canadians would say the line that "divides" the North American continent, thus separating Canada and the United States, is the 49th parallel. Yet, that geographical marker defines about one quarter of the boundary between the two countries. Three quarters of the country lies north of that parallel.

This fact was noted by Anne Marie Owens in "Living in a Parallel Universe," *National Post*, May 17, 2006. "The Maritime provinces, much of Quebec and most of Ontario all lie south of the 49th." She added, "The total length of the boundary between Canada and the United States is 8,893 km. Of that length, only 2,274 km is the 49th parallel." Some cities that lie below the line are Windsor, Toronto, Niagara Falls, Halifax, and St. John's.

The population of Canada is currently 34 million. It is estimated that 19 million Canadians live south of the 49th parallel. Alan Rayburn, an authority on place names, has traced the use of the expression back to 1714 when the Hudson's Bay Company referred to its southern limits as the 49th parallel. To this day, the Canada-U.S. border is conventionally considered to be the 49th parallel.

224. Where will you find the largest dinosaur in the world today?

Prehistoric beasts of the Jurassic period have been extinct for 144 million years, but when you visit Drumheller, Alberta, you can view the world's largest dinosaur. Drumheller is the home of The Royal Tyrrell Museum of Palaeontology, which displays many of the dinosaur fossils that palaeontologists have uncovered in the Badlands of Alberta.

The largest dinosaur is an oversize replica of a female Tyrannosaurus Rex, believed (by Hollywood) to be the most fearsome of the prehistoric beasts. The replica stands outdoors and is 82 feet (24.99 metres) high and 151 feet (46.02 metres) from nose to tail. It is approximately 4.5

times larger than the real thing in its prime. There are 106 stairs inside the body of the beast, and the viewing area, which corresponds to its open, toothed mouth, is 60 square feet and can hold between eight and twelve people at a time.

The framework of the dinosaur is composed of 65,000 pounds of steel. The framework was then covered by wire mesh and sprayed with fibreglass foam. Once the fibreglass hardened, forming the skin of the dinosaur, it was painted and cut into smaller pieces for shipment to the construction site at Drumheller. The individual pieces were fabricated in China and shipped to Drumheller. Amusement Leisure Equipment Limited of Calgary oversaw the project and the assembly. It took nine months to assemble and was officially opened on October 13, 2000, to the continued delight and astonishment of those who visit the Tyrrell Museum.

225. Which is the smallest First Nation?

The origin of the term *First Nations* may be explained by Sol Sanderson, the Saskatchewan elder who was active in the formation of the Assembly of First Nations, which was formed to promote unity among the country's Native groups. One of its position papers quoted him as saying (Internet, November 2006), "By the way, if you ever wondered where that term First Nations came from, I coined it in the early eighties when we were disputing in our forum about our positions on the agenda that we wanted to advance respecting our constitution."

The term was adopted with alacrity and applied across the board, from the largest of the former bands to the smallest, the smallest probably being the Buffalo Point First Nation located in the Lake of the Woods area on the Manitoba-Minnesota border. In 2006 this "nation" of Anishinabe people recorded a population of 125 men, women, and children, fifty-four being status Indians. They have their own language — Chippewa — and a government composed of a hereditary chief with a band council of two members. They reach back in time, but first entered recorded history in the 1700s.

226. Where is Canada Water?

There is no Canada Water in this country, but there is a district with that name in the southeast part of London, England. Canada Water identifies a tube station of the London Underground on the Jubilee Line between Bermondsey and Canary Wharf. The structure, with its distinctive drum shape, was officially opened on September 17, 1999. It meets the needs of commuters who live in the surrounding district of Rotherhithe and of visitors to its well-known wildlife refuge on the River Thames.

227. Where can you view all the players of the Toronto Maple Leafs?

You have to go to the Riverside Gallery in Neustadt, Ontario, the town mainly known as the birthplace of late prime minister John G. Diefenbaker, to see images of all the players of the Toronto Maple Leafs. The Gallery's artist and commercial illustrator Gary McLaughlin, best known as the designer of the distinctive Tim Hortons mug, was commissioned by the company to draw portraits of leading Leafs players. He so enjoyed the undertaking that he decided to paint the heads of all the players in oil on three giant canvases.

The montage is a striking sea of faces. It measures six feet by twelve feet and is titled "Blue Sky — White Snow." The mural received plaudits when it was unveiled at the Ricoh Coliseum in Toronto on March 25, 2008. There are portraits of 747 players, plus images that represent two Leaf logos and the Hockey Hall of Fame. According to Paul Irish in "On the Trial of Some Tasteful Treats," the *Toronto Star*, September 6, 2008, "The work is the first and only piece of sports art to feature every individual who played from the team's inception in 1927 to 2007."

228. Where is the world's oldest baseball diamond?

Baseball may be the national sport of the United States, but it has long been very popular in Canada. According to the *Guinness World Records*,

"The oldest baseball diamond is Labatt Park in London, Ontario, Canada, which was established in 1877 and has hosted baseball games to the present day." In those days, this baseball diamond, or field, was known as Tecumseh Park. The City of London, Ontario, acquired it in 1936, and now it is officially part of Labatt Memorial Park. The claim that it is the oldest such diamond was accepted by the editors of *Guinness World Records* in 2009, after a local group promoted and proved their claim.

The previous title-holder was Fuller Field in Clinton, Massachusetts, which was established in 1878 — one year later. Fuller Field may lack priority but it does claim a distinction: its home plate and bases have purportedly remained in the same location since the year it was opened, whereas the home plate at Labatt Memorial Park has been moved (within the same field) from its original 1877 spot.

229. Is there a monument to a fallen U.S. soldier in Toronto?

No, but there is a monument that depicts a U.S. soldier fallen at the feet of a British soldier, who is standing tall. The monument, known as *Remembering the War of 1812*, was designed by Douglas Coupland, Vancouver's celebrated novelist and sculptor. On November 3, 2008, it was unveiled at 600 Fleet Street on the northwest corner of Lake Shore Boulevard and Bathurst Street in Toronto's Garrison district. It is the result of a private commission from the property developer Malibu Investments. Close by is Fort York National Historic Site, and nearby in Victoria Memorial Square is Walter Allward's monument to the fallen of the War of 1812.

Coupland's monument is quite imaginative, for it consists of two giant toy soldiers on a marble pedestal. The British soldier is wearing the Royal Newfoundland Regiment uniform and he towers over the fallen invader, who wears the uniform of the 16th U.S. Infantry Regiment. Both giant-sized toy soldiers come complete with round bases and symbolic colours: gold for the British, silver for the American. The figures were sculpted in styrofoam over a steel armature and then blanketed with a hard coat of resin.

At the unveiling, Coupland noted, "Toronto exists because of the War of 1812, and Ontario and Canada to a large part exist because of that. It's a war memorial but it's also an incitement for people to remember what's going on in the present as well as in the past."

"Nobody, not even the passing motorists at a busy Toronto intersection, can mistake the message," noted the editorial headed "Public Memory: Brilliant Toy Soldiers" in *The Globe and Mail*, November 5, 2008. "Historical revisions in the U.S. have tried to portray the war's result differently. As Mr. Coupland said: 'I wanted to come up with an elegant and simple way of saying, No, the British won.'" And he succeeded — another battle won!

230. Where do I go to find a replica of the Starship *Enterprise*?

If you fly in a starship, or more likely drive in an automobile, to Vulcan, Alberta, you will find a public replica of the Starship *Enterprise*.

The town of Vulcan has a population of 2,000 people and is located in southern Alberta between the cities of Calgary and Lethbridge. It was so named in 1910 by a CPR surveyor after the Greek god, little knowing that one day Vulcan would be the name given to the "home planet" of Mr. Spock, an extraterrestrial character with pointy ears who was played by actor Leonard Nimoy in the *Star Trek* television series of the 1960s. The citizens of Vulcan decided, for tourism purposes, to make use of the coincidence. Using the name in this way has attracted tourists and bolstered Vulcan's once-failing economy.

The town itself sponsors events that attract youthful fans of the show, who are known as trekkers or trekkies. There are parades, displays, murals, signs, walking tours, Spock Days, the VulCON Star Trek Convention, and so on. The first events were held in the summer of 1993. Two years later a large replica of the Starship *Enterprise* (designated FX6-1995-A) was erected beside the highway that leads to the town. Leonard Nimoy has a standing invitation to visit Vulcan.

231. Which country has the world's longest coastline?

Canada is the second-largest country in the world, but it has the longest coastline of any country, with coasts on three of the world's oceans — the Atlantic, Pacific, and Arctic oceans. The total length of its coastline is 243,791 kilometres. This length is truly astonishing, especially considering that Russia, the world's largest country, has a coastline that is only 37,653 kilometres long. For comparison with two other large countries, the coastline of the United States is 19,942 kilometres, and China's is 14,500 kilometres. The exceptional length of Canada's coastline is explained by the fact that the figure includes the coasts of the islands that comprise the Arctic Archipelago. These northernmost Canadian islands constitute the world's largest group of islands. The group includes six of the world's thirty largest islands, notably Baffin Island, the fifth largest. Thus, much of Canada's coastline lies in the polar region. To put these figures in perspective, the distance from the Earth to the Moon is about 400,000 kilometres, so Canada's combined coastlines stretch a little more than half the distance between our planet and its natural satellite.

232. Is it still the longest undefended border in the world?

It is a commonplace to refer to the Canada–United States border as the longest undefended border in the world. The description dates back to about 1920, but it finally ceased to be true in the year 2007.

At 6,416 kilometres, the border is probably the world's longest international boundary line. Much of it corresponds to the 49th parallel (described in question 224), or at least the southern border does. But there is also the northern border, which separates Alaska from the Yukon Territory and British Columbia, and that stretch of the border is 2,475 kilometres long. So, the total length of the two borders is 8,891 kilometres.

The boundary line is maintained and operated by the Canada Border Services Agency and the United States Customs Service. Until recent years, the border agents, inspectors, and guards on both sides of "the line" went about their work unarmed. After September 11, 2001, U.S. border guards began to carry weapons. In July 2007 Canadian authorities decreed that henceforth its 4,500 border guards would enrol in weapons-training courses and carry firearms. This precaution was taken to deter criminal activity, smuggling, and terrorism.

It is still the world's longest border, but it is no longer undefended.

233. Which is correct: The Niagara Peninsula or the Niagara Frontier?

If there may be said to be a region of Canada that throughout history has been anti-American, it is the part of Southern Ontario called the Niagara Peninsula. The region is regarded as a peninsula in Canada, but in the United States it is known as a frontier. It was mainly settled by Americans who at the time of the American Revolution wished to remain loyal to the British Monarchy and were subsequently called the United Empire Loyalists. It became the scene of battles during the War of 1812, and the invaders were quick to burn the prosperous farms and dwellings that belonged to the Loyalist descendants there.

The irony here is that now this region of Niagara, where there is a profusion of wineries, teems with American tourists who are attracted by the spectacle of Niagara Falls and the spectacular theatrical productions of the Shaw Festival at Niagara-on-the-Lake. Descendants of the original settlers were so fiercely anti-American that they established a public lending library that stocked only Canadian books, the sole such institution in the country.

234. Who "won" on the Plains of Abraham?

The Battle of the Plains of Abraham was originally fought on September 13, 1759. It was won by English forces under the command of General James Wolfe, who were pitted against French forces lead by Major

General Montcalm. As such, it had little to do with Quebec and the rest of Canada. It was a decisive battle, but not the last, because "the other side" won the return engagement the following year at Ste-Foy in Quebec.

The National Battlefields Commission granted permission for the staging of a re-enactment of that epic contest and scheduled it for August 2009. In February, however, it withdrew permission, following protests from the separatist-minded leaders of the Parti Québécois and Bloc Québécois, much to the dismay and disbelief of the rest of Canada.

A good plan for the future would be for the staging of re-enactments on an annual basis — with the English victorious in odd-numbered years, the French victorious in even-numbered years.

235. What is the so-called Ring of Fire?

For many years the term *Ring of Fire* has been used by geologists to refer to a fault-line that corresponds to the coastlines of Southeast Asia. The ring-like region is susceptible to seismic disturbances. In its current Canadian use, the term refers to a massive ore deposit in the James Bay Lowlands of Northern Ontario. The 5,120-square-kilometre area, roughly circular, as if formed by a meteorite, is rich in nickel, copper, gold, and chromite. The region came to public attention on August 28, 2007, when Noront Resources Limited announced the favourable results of exploration diamond drilling. Development of this resource is being challenged by the Native population and environmentalists.

236. What is the Highway of Tears?

In Northern British Columbia, there is a highway that links the cities of Prince George and Prince Rupert. It is called Yellowhead Highway 16 and is deserted for much of its 720 kilometres. Since 1974, more than a dozen lone females, mainly young women of aboriginal background, have gone missing or have been murdered along this route.

These disappearances and unsolved murders may be the work of a single serial killer or that of different murders. In the 1990s the highway acquired the unofficial designation as the "Highway of Tears."

237. What is the Highway of Heroes?

A 172-kilometre stretch of Highway 401 that crosses Southern Ontario was designated the Highway of Heroes (*Autoroute des héros*). The designation was made by the Ontario Ministry of Transport on August 24, 2007. The newly named section of the busy throughway extends from Glen Miller Road at Trenton to the Don Valley Parkway of Toronto. Along the route, signs that depict shields and red poppies honour Canada's fallen servicemen and women, mainly those who served in Afghanistan, whose remains are conveyed by hearses in military cortèges from Canadian Forces Base Trenton to the forensic centre in downtown Toronto. In 1970 it was noted that family members and friends would gather on bridges and overpasses to mark the passage of their loved ones. Some people would salute, others would stand at stiff attention. Still others would hold erect Canadian flags.

The idea of honouring the war dead was urged by reporter Pete Fisher in his article "Highway of Heroes: Let's Make It Official," which appeared in the Cobourg *Daily Star* on July 13, 2007. He wrote, "What began quietly, spontaneously in Northumberland County has now extended along the 172 kilometres, or 107 miles, of Highway 401 travelled by repatriated Canadian soldiers killed in Afghanistan. People standing on bridges have become a powerful expression of support by fellow Canadians for the troops and their families."

Fisher credits *Toronto Sun* columnist Joe Warmington with the coinage of the phrase "Highway of Heroes" on June 25, 2007. With Fisher's help, the unofficial designation took on an official life of its own, despite objections based on the fact that the war dead are combatants — and brave ones at that — but not necessarily heroes.

238. What are Jane's Walks?

Jane's Walks were named after Jane Jacobs (1916–2006), the urban writer and social activist, whose strong convictions about the "livable" cities have been highly influential. In 1968, protesting the Vietnam War, she left New York City with her family and settled in Toronto, where she was immediately celebrated for her views on the delights of urban life and the perils of civic planning. She did much to stopping developers from turning Toronto into an "unlivable" city.

Inspired by her contribution, a group called Centre for City Ecology dedicated its efforts to the encouragement of "walkable neigh-bourhoods, urban literacy, and cities planned for people." To this end, it sponsors cultural walking tours of the city's diverse neighbourhoods, calling them "Jane's Walks." Twenty-seven such tours, led by specialists or students, were first held on "Jane Jacobs Day," May 5, 2007. Judged to be a great success, the idea spread to New York City and then to cities across Canada.

239. Where in the country will you find Eilean a' Phrionnsa?

You will find it in the Gulf of St. Lawrence. *Eilean a' Phrionnsa* is the officially recognized name of Prince Edward Island in Scottish Gaelic. The province's official name in French is *Île-du-Prince-Edouard*. So, including its familiar English name, the province has three official names.

240. Which is larger, Prince Edward Island or Rhode Island?

Prince Edward Island is the smallest province of Canada, and Rhode Island is the smallest state of the United States. Surprisingly, P.E.I. is about twice as large as R.I. The official figures are as follows: P.E.I.'s size is 5,683.91 square kilometres, or 2,194.57 square miles. R.I.'s size is 3,140 square kilometres, or 1,214 square miles.

241. Which days are the snowiest?

The short answer to that question is "winter days."

Here is the long answer: If you visit Canada and want to see snow, some days are better than others. Climatologists' records show that you are most likely to encounter heavy snow during winter in Toronto on a Thursday, but least likely to encounter it in on a Sunday. For Vancouver, heavy snows are tend to fall on Saturday and are least likely on Tuesday. For Montreal, Saturday is the best day for heavy snow, while Monday the best day for light snow.

242. What is the coldest capital city in the world?

It is generally agreed that the world's coldest capital — after Ulan Bator in Mongolia — is Ottawa, Canada. Ottawa's average January temperature is -6.3 degrees Celsius during the day, -15.5 degrees Celsius during the night. (In July the temperature rises to 26.4 degrees during the day, 15.1 degrees during the night.) The average annual snowfall is 221.5 centimetres.

things

243. What would Alberto Manguel deposit in his own national "time capsule"?

Alberto Manguel, the Argentine-born essayist and anthologist who settled in Canada — though he now lives in France — responded to the challenge of an exhibition in Paris called Visions of the Future to develop his own national "time capsule" to conserve the dreams of contemporary Canadians for far-future generations.

He wrote about his response in "Ghosts of the Future: Unborn Dreams," the *Globe and Mail*, October 28, 2000. Here is what he said:

> I'd like to think that the list would be wonderfully eclectic: the petroglyphs in the Saskatchewan prairie that hold messages yet to be deciphered; the tent in Auschwitz where the stolen belongings of the inmates were kept and which was known as "Kanada"; Pierre Trudeau's brave Constitution for a country he believed should stand firmly on its own; the failed Finnish project of Sointula that attempted to set up a socialist society in a coastal village in British Columbia; Margaret Atwood's cautionary novel *The Handmaid's Tale*; the perfect reading space of Toronto's Metro Library, one of the strongholds of our collective memories; the all-encompassing theatre of Robert Lepage, redefining the roles of the actor and the audience; David Suzuki's repeated warnings of future ecological devastation; Norman Bethune's work in China, foreshadowing the concept of *Médecines sans frontières*; the 1999 Nunavut Act that holds in these desperate times an almost utopian promise that might just be fulfilled.

244. What is the colour of your passport?

There is a colour code for Canadian passports.

Your passport is green if you are a member of the Privy Council, a member of Parliament, a provincial premier, or a provincial cabinet minister. Your passport is red in colour if you are a member of the diplomatic corps. If you are none of the above, like the vast majority of Canadians, your passport is blue in colour.

245. How many Canadians hold dual citizenship?

The Canadian Citizenship Act was amended in 1977 to recognize "dual citizenship" and even "multiple citizenship." Wide-spread migration and immigration, coupled with globalization, trade, and economic pacts (like the European Union), are factors that have led most countries of the world to recognize the fact that some of their citizens (whether native-born or nationalized) are also recognized to be citizens of other countries. They may hold valid dual or multiple passports. In 2005 there were estimated to be 691,000 Canadians who were also citizens of other countries, 6,000 of them citizens of more than two countries. It is noted that the Queen Elizabeth II holds Canadian citizenship as well as sixteen other citizenships. The subject came to public attention in August 2005, when it was noted that the governor general-designate, Michaëlle Jean, a native of Haiti, was both a citizen of France through marriage and a citizen of Canada through naturalization. Lynda Hurst, "Duelling Opinions over Dual Citizenship," the *Toronto Star*, August 20, 2005.

246. Did a Canadian invent the flight recorder?

It was not the flight recorder — the so-called black box that records what malfunctioned on a plane that crashed — that was invented by a Canadian, but the Crash Position Indicator, known as the CPI. Both inventions have been important in civil and military aviation.

The Alberta-born electrical engineer named Harry Stevinson — who was associated with the National Research Council and spells his name this way! — developed a mobile radio beacon that rides near the tail of an aircraft. The beacon takes the form of a "tumbling aerofoil" that weighs only five kilograms. It is a tiny radio transmitter with its own battery, micro-circuitry, and antenna. Its spring-loaded release mechanism is activated upon impact, and it then broadcasts the location of the downed craft.

Stevinson produced the first working model in the 1960s and Leigh Instruments manufactured them, according to Roy Mayer, writing in *Scientific Canadian: Invention and Innovation from Canada's National Research Council* (1960).

247. Is there a building in Ottawa designed to resemble the Sphinx?

As unlikely as it may seem, there is indeed a government building in Ottawa that was designed to resemble, in outline, Egypt's Great Sphinx at Giza.

The structure, located at 125 Sussex Drive, is the Lester B. Pearson Building, named for the late prime minster and Nobel Peace laureate. The structure was opened in 1973 to house the federal government departments that are now known as Foreign Affairs and International Trade.

In August 1973, Queen Elizabeth II had this to say about Pearson: "Lester Pearson's great qualities were that he was considerate, tolerant and fair, and he had an infectious cheerfulness and optimism. If the atmosphere of this building can come to reflect those qualities, it could not be a better inspiration for the people who work here."

There is a paradox here. Pearson was accessible and easygoing, whereas the building — dubbed "Fort Pearson" — strikes the passerby, if not the member of these departments, as somewhat remote and inscrutable. Like the Great Sphinx, however, the structure houses a great many secrets. Indeed, the building has been dubbed "Fort Pearson."

Here are further details from the Government of Canada's website (August 30, 2008): "Designed by Brian Brooks of the architectural firm Webb, Zerafa, Menkes, the Lester B. Pearson Building has a tiered structure designed to evoke strength, history and a bond with past civilizations. Its four towers covered in granite aggregate provide some 56,000 metres of office space and are connected by an enclosed glass lobby. In 1998, it received the Best Government Building Award from the Building Owners' and Managers' Association of Canada."

248. Did a Canadian invent the first Walkie-Talkie?

The short answer to that question is "yes." The long answer is that the Canadian in question might best be described as a pioneer or a developer rather than an inventor because, as usual, there are rival claimants in other countries.

What is not disputed is that in 1937 Donald Lewes Hings (1907–2004), a wireless engineer with Consolidated Mining and Smelting Company in Nelson, British Columbia, devised an advanced, mobile, two-way radio communication system for the use of the company's prospectors and miners. With the outbreak of the Second World War, Hings joined the National Research Council and in 1940 developed a smaller unit, which he called the "Pack Set." It was intended for the use of the Canadian Military, and tens of thousands of units were produced. As bulky as a briefcase, the unit was again destined to be reduced in size — the next year, as it turned out. This more compact unit was called the C-18.

The following event occurred in 1941 (to quote a subsequent account) when Mr. Hings was demonstrating the device in Toronto: "A reporter saw a soldier walking about with the C-18 version strapped to his uniform. 'What does it do?' the soldier was asked. 'Well, you can talk with it while you walk with it,' was the answer and the name Walkie-Talkie was born. The technology was adopted by both Canadian and United States troops during World War II and was essential for their air-to-ground and land-to-sea communications." This is said to mark the coinage of the term *Walkie-Talkie*, despite the fact that the first patent he filed was for the "Walkie-Talkie" (so designated) on October 7, 1940.

Hings, an originator of fifty-five patents in Canada and the United States, received many awards, including a Member of the Order of the British Empire. He subsequently developed the C-27, which resembles the image of the Walkie-Talkie often seen in Second World War movies, though Hings preferred to call it the Handi-Talkie.

249. Did a Canadian invent the "wrist radio"?

Nostalgia buffs often assume that the "wrist radio" was the invention of cartoonist Chester Gould, as the radio was worn by his fictional detective Dick Tracy in the comic strip of the same name, which was wildly popular in the late 1940s and early 1950s. But it seems that the "wrist radio" — along with the original walkie-talkie and the primitive pager (earmarked for medical doctors) — are all the inventions of an engineer named Al Gross.

Born in Toronto, raised in Cleveland, Ohio, Gross graduated in electrical engineering from today's Case Western Reserve University. For the U.S. military's Office of Strategic Services, he developed the ground-to-air, battery-operated radio that could transmit and receive up to 50 kilometres. He developed the first pager in 1949 and two years later the first cell phone. In 1959 he worked on timing devices for Titan, Atlas, and Minuteman missiles.

His contribution to pop culture came in the late 1940s, when Dick Tracy cartoonist Chester Gould visited the Gross workshop. Mr. Gould saw two items that sparked a brainstorm: a watch with a built-in beeper and a wireless microphone.

"Can I use this?" he asked the inventor, who agreed to the request.

In 1949, the comic-strip detective made his debut as a crime fighter aided by a two-way "wrist radio."

Unknown or at least unrecognized by historians of inventions in his native Canada, Al Gross died in Sun City, Arizona, aged 82, on December 21, 2000.

Many a youngster who read comic books — like the present author — yearned for his own wrist radio. Today it exists, of course, in the form of the cell phone.

250. Did a Canadian invent the Whoopee Cushion?

The earliest known rubber cushion that, when compressed, emits the sound of flatulence, was manufactured and marketed by JEM Rubber Co. of Toronto. According to joke-and-prank collector Derek McCormack, writing in "Making Whoopee," *National Post*, March 29, 2008, "In the late 1920s, it moulded an inflatable bag that farted. Possibly it was meant to be a balloon."

In 1930 the company approached S.S. Adams Co. of Asbury Park, New Jersey. S.S. Adams Co. was known as a maker of gags, pranks, and other practical jokes, and it was hoped that they would distribute the novelty item in the United States. Soren S. Adams declined the offer, but he changed his mind when the Toronto company was able to manufacture the rubber inflatable device and sell it through his rival, Johnson Smith and Company.

Adams introduced his own version called the Razzberry Cushion, which continues to sell to this day. During the Depression, the device sold for twenty-five cents, with a premium version available for a dollar and a quarter. In 1944 JEM Rubber Co. was purchased by the Dayton Rubber Company of Dayton, Ohio, which seems to have dropped the item from its line of goods.

The Whoopie Cushion has been sold under a variety of names: Boop-Boob A Doop, Oh-Oh Pillow, Musical Cushion, Bronx Cheer, Natural's Rival, and Flarp. It is still available in novelty shops in tourist sections of town. Its Canadian origin was unsuspected until McCormack wrote his article. Another Canadian first! (Who says Canadians do not blow their own horns?)

251. What were the "Christie comedies"?

The "Christie comedies" were domestic comedies released in the last years of the silent era and in the early years of the sound era. They were created by Christie Comedies, a movie company founded in Hollywood in 1915 by the Christie brothers, who acted as producers and directors.

The two brothers, both born in London, Ontario, were Albert (Al) Christie (1886–1951) and Charles H. Christie (1880–1955). They released such "domestic comedies" as *Charley's Aunt* (1925, 1930), *Up in Mabel's Room* (1926), and *Tillie's Punctured Romance* (1928).

Film historians rank the Christie brothers' work on the level of Mack Sennett (another former Canadian) and Hal Roach. They credit the Christies with working out the formula for the "domestic comedy," wherein the action moves from the parlour to the pantry to the bedroom. In the words of the obituary writer of *Variety*, "The brothers were hard hit in the depression and Charles went into the real-estate business."

252. Was Rameses I, Pharaoh of Egypt, ever in Canada?

It is hard to believe that the mummified remains of Rameses I, Pharaoh of Ancient Egypt, were displayed for 140 years in a glass-enclosed cabinet at the Daredevil Museum at Niagara Falls, Ontario. Few sightseers who passed that cabinet and stared at the partly decomposed mummy appreciated that it was the regal remains of the once-mighty Pharaoh Rameses I, the founder of the 19th Dynasty in 1293 B.C. as well as the progenitor of an illustrious line of kings who unified their divided country.

As one commentator has written of Rameses: "His official title before becoming king was Master of Horse, Commander of the Fortress, Controller of the Nile Mouth, Charioteer of His Majesty, King's Envoy to Every Foreign Land, Royal Scribe, Colonel, and General of the Lord of the Two Lands." Once upon the throne, he had even more titles and was even more powerful!

In 1860, grave robbers sold his mummy for seven English pounds to James Douglas, a distinguished physician and surgeon from Montreal. Douglas had made the purchase on behalf of Colonel Sidney Barnett, the son of Thomas Barnett, who is known as the entrepreneurial founder and proprietor of the Niagara Museum, a once-popular tourist attraction in Niagara Falls, Ontario. In 1827 Thomas Barnett had opened his museum as a "cabinet of curiosities" at Table Rock, overlooking the mighty cataracts of Niagara. It was the first museum in the land that was to become Canada, and one of the earliest museums in North America.

As one commentator expressed it, the remains of Rameses were "exhibited alongside such displays as those of a two-headed calf and a five-legged pig." The museum, with its varied collection of natural and man-made artifacts, passed through a number of hands. It came to be regarded as tacky and fell on hard times, only to be closed for good in 1999. All the artifacts were acquired by William Jamieson, a Toronto collector and dealer in ancient and tribal art, who sold the royal mummy — plus an assortment of 145 artifacts that came with the original purchase — to the Michael C. Carlos Museum of Emory University in Atlanta, Georgia. Once there, carbon-dating and other considerations established the early date of the mummy and its "royal" status. Despite paying $2 million for the collection, in 2003 Emory University donated it all to the Supreme Council of Antiquities in Cairo. The Supreme Council has long been active in repatriating national treasures; it still hopes the British Museum will "return" the Rosetta Stone.

So Rameses I, after a relatively short visit on the shores of the Niagara River, has been returned to the land of his birth. The royal mummy is on display at the Mummification Museum in the city of Luxor, overlooking the banks of the Nile River in Egypt, oblivious of its sojourn so near the mighty Falls of Niagara.

253. Have you heard the "Micma'q Honour Song"?

The "Micma'q Honour Song" is a contemporary chant popular with such choral groups as the Toronto Children's Chorus. It was composed and arranged in 2000 by Lydia Adams, a native of Glace Bay, N.S. Here is a short description of the very composition, from the program "The Magic of Music: 2008–2009 Concert Season," of that chorus: "The Micma'q Honour Song is a chant dedicated to the honour of the Creator. The use of nature sounds and the call of the human voice honour this tradition of the Micma'q peoples of eastern North America. With choristers surrounding the audience as in a darkened forest, a clustered hum and the sound of blowing wind are followed by the distant call of a loon. The elemental beat of a drum and the haunting two-part Micma'q chant continue as the sounds of chipmunk, wolf, owl, songbird, and finally loon draw the song to its close." Everyone should have the opportunity to hear this appealing choral composition.

254. What is the Canadian connection of Hallmark cards?

Familiar to most North Americans are "Hallmark cards" (those ubiquitous greeting cards) and "The Hallmark Hall of Fame" (the once-popular radio and television drama series). These are the products of Hallmark Cards Inc., a giant card production-and-distribution operation launched in 1910 by Joyce Clyde Hall. From a stationery store in Kansas City, Missouri, he sold postcards; when they went out of fashion, he sold greeting cards and then began to design, print, and distribute them.

In 1931 Hallmark Cards came to an agreement with William E. Coutts Company Ltd. This Toronto company was established around 1920 for the manufacture and distribution of Canadian cards by the businessman W.E. Coutts. The agreement called for the joint distribution in Canada of the cards produced by William E. Coutts Company Ltd. For some years these cards were known throughout the Canadian greeting-card industry as "Coutts Hallmark." The association, based on a handshake, became the first of many international ventures for Hallmark Cards. In 1958 the Coutts company was acquired by the American giant, which by its 50th anniversary, in

1960, was producing four million cards a day to meet international demand.

255. What is the Golden Rule Poster?

The Golden Rule Poster has the so-called Golden Rule expressed in the words of the texts of thirteen of the world's largest faith groups. The attractive, four-colour poster measures 22 inches by 29 inches and is regularly seen in schools and places of worship.

At the centre of the poster is an image of the planet Earth, with the words "The Golden Rule" in yellow type. Radiating from the central circle are thirteen smaller circles, all of equal size, which represent the world's leading religions and religious philosophies. These are, in alphabetical order, Baha'i Faith, Buddhism, Christianity, Confucianism, Hinduism, Islam, Jainism, Judaism, Native Spirituality, Sikhism, Taoism, Unitarianism, and Zoroastrianism.

If you ask most people to recite the Golden Rule, and you will probably hear something to the effect of: "Do unto others as you would have them do unto you." As surprising as it may seem, this idea lies at the heart of most of the world's great religious and spiritual traditions. The Golden Rule may be philosophically described as the Ethic of Reciprocity or the Principle of Mutuality. It should be a personal maxim. If only its injunction were put into practice!

The value of a poster that featured this message occurred to Paul McKenna, director of the interfaith department with the Scarboro Mission Society, a Canadian Roman Catholic organization that for many years has operated from its headquarters in Scarborough in the east end of Toronto. McKenna researched the text and commissioned artist Kathy VanLoon Gillis to design the arresting poster. The mission society, which printed and published it in July 2000, was gratified to find that it was well received in educational and interfaith circles from the first. It has been widely distributed in English and other languages. The Scarboro Mission has established websites with the message of the poster, which constitutes a unique Canadian contribution to ecumenical unity, interfaith harmony, as well as world peace.

256. Does the American flag fly over the Centre Block on Parliament Hill on the two-dollar bill?

The Stars and Stripes, the U.S. flag, does not fly over Parliament Hill in Ottawa. Yet there was an urban rumour that the flag depicted on the old $2, $5, and $10 Canadian banknotes was not the Maple Leaf Flag but the Stars and Stripes. The rumour began to circulate with the introduction of the new $5 bill in May 1986. Soon people were examining the outline of the Parliament Buildings with magnifying glasses to scrutinize the tiny image of the flag flying from the top of the Centre Block.

What they saw was not the Maple Leaf flag, but the Red Ensign, which bears a surface resemblance to the U.S. flag. The Red Ensign has the Union Jack in the upper left-hand corner and this was confused with the field of stars that occupies the same position on the U.S. flag. The Red Ensign was flown until replaced by the Maple Leaf flag in 1965, and this was in keeping with the "period" images of Sir Wilfrid Laurier on the $5 bill and of Sir John A. Macdonald on the $10 bill. So the Stars and Stripes never flew over Parliament Hill. Nor did any image of it appear on Canadian banknotes.

257. Does the loonie appear in a *Star Trek* episode?

As unlikely as it might seem, the loonie — the Canadian one-dollar coin — was featured in an episode of the *Star Trek: Deep Space Nine* series. The episode was called "Blaze of Glory," and it was aired on May 12, 1997. In this episode, the character Michael Eddington (played by Kenneth Marshall), a former Star Fleet commander, boasted of having a family heirloom in the form of a twenty-second century Canadian one-dollar coin, which he called his "lucky loonie."

This is an uncanny pre-configuration of the tradition of the "lucky loonie" in world hockey tournaments. During the 2002 Winter

Olympics at Salt Lake City, a Canadian icemaker for ice hockey tournament buried a loonie under centre ice. The tradition continued with the IIHF World Hockey Championships between Canada and Sweden at Helsinki in 2003. Loonies have been buried beneath centre ice ever since. Even the Royal Canadian Mint entered the fray and began issuing a specially designed "lucky loonie" each year for the summer and winter games.

258. Is there a "lost loonie"?

There is no "lost loonie," but the dies used for first golden-coloured coin were lost or stolen in transit between Ottawa, where the dies were cut, and Winnipeg, where the coins were to be stamped. As one commentator has written, "The design for the coin was meant to be a *voyageur* theme, similar to the country's previous one dollar / silver dollar coin, but the master dies, created in Ottawa, were lost by the courier service while in transit to the Royal Canadian Mint in Winnipeg. In order to avoid possible counterfeiting, a different design was used."

Had the dies not been lost or stolen, the inaugural coin would have featured a voyageur and never been nicknamed the loonie at all.

259. What are the two most "prized pucks"?

A puck is a puck, but when it is shot into the other team's net, it acquires a special significance and is often put on public display. Sometimes it travels across the country to augment displays — this has been the fate of two special pucks.

The first highly valued puck was the one shot into the Soviet Team's net by Team Canada's Paul Henderson. The goal was scored in the eighth and last game, which was a tiebreaker in the Summit Series played in Moscow on September 29, 1972. The puck is now a valued exhibit at the Hockey Hall of Fame in Toronto.

The second special puck ended up in the opponent's net, bring about Team Canada's overtime victory against the U.S. team. It has been described as Sidney Crosby's "golden goal." The win took place during overtime play at the Vancouver Winter Olympics, February 28, 2010.

This puck later found its way into the duffel-bag of Stefan Fonselius, a linesman who worked the Olympic final between Canada and the United States. He took it with him from Vancouver to Montreal, Frankfurt, Helsinki, and his hometown of Turku. Its return journey was by mail to Switzerland and then to Toronto, where it was placed on display at the Hockey Hall of Fame, March 17, 2010, immediately becoming the signature attraction.

260. Who invented the jockstrap and the goalie pad?

The athletic support for men, also known as the jockstrap, was invented by Jack Cartledge of the Elastic Hosiery Company in Guelph, Ontario. According to Ken Lefolii, writing in *Weekend*, June 16, 1979, Cartledge devised the support in 1920 and patented it in 1923, marketing it under the trade name Protex 13.

Goalie pads are said to be the invention of the hockey enthusiast Emil "Pop" Kenesky of Hamilton, in 1926. His handmade pads were able to stop slapshots travelling at 90 miles per hour. Even in his nineties, he was making three hundred sets of pads a year.

261. What are the ingredients of Voyageurs' Punch?

The voyageurs of old, who were engaged in the fur trade, knew nothing of the Voyageurs' Punch. The cocktail owes its popularity to modern-day voyageurs — wilderness canoeists who retrace the trails of the early explorers for recreation.

Wilderness canoeing was popularized in 1952 by Eric W. Morse, an Ottawa-based historian and canoeing enthusiast. It was while exploring the Churchill River in 1955 that Voyageurs' Punch was developed. As Morse recalled in *Freshwater Saga: Memoirs of a Lifetime of Wilderness Canoeing in Canada* (1987), "It did not take us long to evolve what we considered the best rum cocktail: a daiquiri made by adding lemon powder, sugar, and water, which has now become well-known among Canadian canoeists as 'voyageurs' punch.' It has the delightful property of making one oblivious to the bugs, although there is one theory that the lemon actually drives the bugs away." There was no chance that any canoeist in Morse's party would ever become an alcoholic, as each participant was limited to two ounces of rum a day!

262. What is icewine?

Icewine (spelled as one word) is a premium wine produced in the Niagara Peninsula. "The grapes are left on the vine into early winter, usually until late December or early January. They are picked at night with the temperatures at -8 degrees [Celsius] so the grapes stay frozen. The temperature is critical because it freezes the water in the grape but not the inner nectar. The grape presses, which are usually moved outside to maintain the cold condition, gently squeeze the grapes as they are brought in from the field. Not much syrup emerges, but it is oh so rich!" So wrote Hans and Allyson Tammemgi in *Exploring Niagara: The Complete Guide to Niagara Falls and Vicinity* (1997). Icewine is expensive to produce and is sold in small, 375-millitre bottles. It serves as an ideal dessert wine.

263. What is ice cider?

Ice cider is a delicious dessert wine with a taste that has been compared to that of a rich crème brûlée. As a food product, it resembles icewine, another Canadian innovation as described in the preceding question.

Ice cider, like regular cider, is prepared from apples. It takes about eighty apples to produce a half-bottle of ice cider. The juice comes from apples that are harvested in the fall after the first frost. In some instances, apples are picked off the branches while still frozen. The period of fermentation is nine months, and the resulting ice cider reaches an alcohol level of about 12 percent. A bottle of cider is affordable, for it sells at about half the price of icewine.

"Ice cider is poised to take its place alongside maple syrup, tourière and butter tarts as one of Canada's most popular contributions to the world of gastronomy," wrote Chris Johns in "A Cold Shower for Hot Cider," *Saturday Night*, February 2005.

The notion of using apples rather than grapes in the production of wine first occurred to Christian Barthomeuf, a French vintner who had immigrated to Canada in 1979. In the mid-1990s, he founded his own winery at Hemmingford in Quebec's Eastern Townships. Reasoning that apples have a longer growing season than grapes and are less vulnerable to cold weather, he focused on producing a cider-like wine, using McIntoshes (tart) and Spartan (sweet). The first ice cider was bottled by Domaine Pinncale in the year 2000. Ice cider from this winery and from other boutique wineries is now available in most provinces and in many countries. Production takes place in wineries in Quebec, Ontario, Alberta, and British Columbia.

264. What is Baby Duck?

Baby Duck is the brand name of a pop wine with a low (7 percent) alcoholic content. In 1971 it was introduced to the market by Andrès, an inventive winery located in the Niagara Peninsula. The following year its cousin, Cold Duck, with a higher alcoholic content, was also introduced. The lighter version quickly became Ontario's largest-selling wine.

265. What are the three most-acclaimed Canadian films of all time?

What a difficult question to answer!

Nanook of the North is probably the most acclaimed Canadian motion picture of all time. It was set and shot in the Eastern Arctic, and it covers the daily life of an Eskimo family. What could be more Canadian than that? It was directed by documentary filmmaker Robert Flaherty in 1922, and its ambience was recreated in 1994 as *Kabloonak (Nanook)*, a dramatic film directed by Claude Massot, with Charles Dance and other professional actors.

In the modern period, however, there are two dramatic feature films that were written, produced, and directed by the consummate filmmaker Denys Arcand that rise head and shoulders above all the rest. The first of these is *The Decline of the American Empire* (1986). As film critic Gerald Pratley noted, "The conversation is witty, sharp, funny, furious, bright and bitchy. The film is a triumph for the players and Denys Arcand. It brought him the recognition at home and abroad he so richly deserved after making many distinguished but less-noticed movies."

Arcand went on to produce its sequel, *The Barbarian Invasions* (2003). Pratley described it as one of "the truly great films of our time." He added, "It is nostalgic, bittersweet, and satiric yet wise about love and life, vice and virtue, politics and pretentiousness. It is all Arcand, with his humour, charm, and clear-minded intellectual expressionism. And behind it all, we can imagine his serious creativity, mixed with his spontaneous laughter and sense of enjoyment."

According to the same critic, writing in *A Century of Canadian Cinema* (2003), the two films focus on the lives of a group of male and female university professors who meet for dinner and talk about sex and sociology, their personal relationships and private fantasies.

Arcand's films are Quebec films before they are Canadian films or American films, yet their appeal is universal. Both films critically yet affectionately depict human relationships against the backdrop of American values and Western civilization, within the context of Quebec's society.

266. What are the names of some board games devised by Canadians?

Some board games devised by Canadians are identified in *Canada Firsts* (1992), written by U.S. consumer critic Ralph Nader with the research of Nadia Milleron and Duff Conacher. Here are some of the games they name:

Trivial Pursuit was developed in 1979–81 by Chris Haney and Scott Abbott of Toronto.

Yachtzee was developed in the 1800s by a wealthy Canadian couple on their yacht, so they called it "The Yacht Game"; they sold the rights in the 1920s, and the name was changed to the now-familiar Yachtzee.

Balderdash was introduced in 1984 by Laura Robinson and Paul Toyne of Toronto.

An Evening of Murder was introduced in 1986 by crime reporter Max Haines.

Supremacy was introduced in 1984 by Robert J Simpson of Toronto — it's a game about the world's superpowers.

A Question of Scruples was introduced in 1985 by Henry Makow, a writer and former professor in Winnipeg.

Pictionary was introduced in 1986 by Rob Angel of Vancouver.

Ultimatum was introduced in 1985 by Fred Bates of Hamilton.

These board and card games are something for families and friends to do during Canada's long winter nights!

267. What is *Pikaia gracilens?*

During the Cambrian era some 530 million years ago, the Burgess Shale was a seabed that teemed with exotic forms of aquatic life that are now extinct. Today the shale, located in British Columbia's Yoho National Park, is designated a UNESCO World Heritage Site. It is the site of extensive quarrying by scientists.

One of the most amazing life forms preserved in fossil form in the shale here is the worm-like creature named *Pikaia gracilens*. The fauna measures about three centimetres in length and looks a little like a wiggling minnow. As for its designation, Pikaia is pronounced "pihKAYah" and was named after a nearby mountain; *gracilens* is Latin for "graceful." In its day, Pikaia may well have exhibited graceful movements.

Pikaia is significant in evolutionary history. Paleontologists recognize it to be a primitive chordate; indeed, it is the earliest known representative of the phylum to which we, as creatures with backbones, belong. Pikaia is described as the founder of the phylum Chordata.

Stephen Jay Gould waxed eloquent about Pikaia's significance and importance in his book *Wonderful Life: The Burgess Shale and the Nature of History* (1989). On one of its pages appears a pen-and-ink drawing of the living fauna by Marianne Collins, an artist and illustrator with the Royal Ontario Museum.

Every two years since 2002, the Paleontology Division of the Geological Association of Canada makes a presentation to recognize a recent contribution to outstanding research in Canadian paleontology it is called the Pikaia Award.

268. What does Tiktaalik tell us about early life on Earth?

Tiktaalik roseae (its scientific name) is a transitional creature — half-fish, half mammal — that existed during the Devonian era. It was found in 2006 in fossil form on Ellesmere Island, Nunavut, by a team scientists from the University of Chicago. The team spent five summers in their search for a creature that could thrive in shallow waters some 375 million years ago, when the High Arctic enjoyed a tropical rather than an arctic climate.

The scientific article announcing this important scientific discovery, titled "A Devonian Tetrapod-like Fish and the Evolution of the Tetrapod Body Plan," appeared in *Nature*, April 6 2006, and was signed by evolutionary biologists Edward B. Daeschler, Neil H. Shubin, and Farish A. Jenkins. Inuit elders recommended that the scientists call the fish-like creature with both fins and legs *Tiktaalik*, the Inuktitut word for burbot, a freshwater codfish.

Tiktaalik is a intermediate, amphibious life form, and while it "tells us" nothing at all, being extinct, its existence, anticipated by evolutionary biologists, could be seen as something of a "missing link" between those forms that thrived in water and those that thrived on land. By this measure, Tiktaalik shows evolution in action.

269. What is the "Humble" telescope?

The Canadian-designed space telescope that was launched into orbit in 2003 is technically known as MOST (Microvariability and Oscillations of Stars Space Telescope). This fifteen-centimetre optical telescope is a suitcase-sized instrument and hence quite "humble" in size and cost, so it is referred to as the Humble telescope. It is able to centre on a single star for two months while orbiting 820 kilometres above the Earth, and it is powerful enough to detect changes in that star. Built by Dynacon Inc., a Toronto high-tech company that specializes in automation and robotics, it was assembled at the University of Toronto's Institute for Aerospace Studies and was underwritten by the Canadian Space Agency. It cost $10 million compared to the $2 billion outlay for NASA's Hubble Space Telescope. The Humble was designed to search for extrasolar, Earth-sized planets in the so-called Goldilocks zone (where it's neither too hot nor too cold). This is from Peter Calamai in "Canada Leads Cosmic Search for a New Earth," the *Toronto Star*, January 12, 2005.

270. Did a Canadian company invent the personal computer?

The answer to this question is yes, if any single company is to be credited with the invention of the personal computer. That company is MCM Micro Computer Machines Inc. of Kingston, Ontario. Mainframe computers were in use by corporations by the 1960s, but the notion that an ordinary person might want to own his or her personal computer was a notion that was still in the future.

The first personal computer was the MCM/70 Microcomputer, because it had its own built-in microprocessor. In other words, it was not attached to a mainframe. It was designed, built, manufactured, advertised, marketed, and sold to individuals for personal use and was unveiled in Toronto on September 25, 1973, two years ahead of the trendsetting Apple 1 PC.

The MCM/70 was pretty primitive in comparison with its successors. It boasted 8 kilobytes of RAM and used a tape drive for storage. It was designed and produced by Mers Kutt, a computer specialist, to replace the punch cards that were still being used at Queen's University, in Kingston, Ontario, where he was employed at the time. He then formed his own company, Micro Computer Machines Inc., to manufacture and market it.

"The MCM/70 could be described as the Avro Arrow of computing history. It was truly ahead of its time and showed lots of promise, but never quite took off because, at least in part, it was made in Canada — far from computing's heartland," according to Rachel Ross in "Remembering the MCM/70," the *Toronto Star*, September 25, 2003. The MCM/70's pre-eminent position in the world of personal computing is recognized by the journal *IEEE Annals of the History of Computing*.

271. What was the significance of the Commodore PET?

The Commodore PET is considered by many industry observers to be the world's first personal computer. It was demonstrated in January 1977 at the Consumer Electronics Show in Chicago, Illinois, months before the release of the Apple II and the Radio Shack TRS80. It was described as "fully functional out of the box." It had a nine-inch, blue-and-white monitor, and 4 kilobytes of memory, though there was room for additional memory. It used the Commodore BASIC Operating System, written by Bill Gates and Paul Allen from their fledgling

Micro-Soft Corporation (they later dropped the hyphen to make it a single word). Its design and development in Toronto was overseen by entrepreneur Jack Tramiel.

One historian wrote, "There are several rumours about the source of the name PET. Officially it was an acronym for Personal Electronic Transactor, but PET are also the initials of one of Jack Tramiel's relatives (his wife, it is said). Whatever the origin, Jack thought that PET sounded better and would have some positive linkage with the Pet Rock fad of the late 1970s. Faced with intense competition, the company folded in 1986."

272. Were Crocs devised or developed in Canada?

The answer is that they were both devised and developed in Canada, though the information is somewhat scant.

Crocs are lightweight, slip-resistant, non-marking, multicoloured, form-adjusting, casual-style footwear. They are moulded from "croslite" and slope upwards like a crocodile's snout, hence its catchy trade name. Croslite is ethylene vinyl acetate.

The Croc was first trademarked in the United States by Crocs, a company founded by three friends — Scott Seamans, George Boedecker, and Lyndon Hanson, all of Boulder, Colorado. On a vacation in the Caribbean, they saw an early clog (half sandal, half Dutch-style clog) that had been designed and manufactured by Foam Creations Inc., of Quebec City, a research-intensive company that devised methods of using injection moulding expanded ethylene-based foams. The three businessmen, sensing a marketing opportunity, acquired the rights to the process, added a strap to the back of the cog, bright colours, and gave it the catchy, child-friendly name Croc.

Their first batch of Crocs were sold in July 2002, largely to boaters and outdoors people. The Beach model caught on at the Fort Lauderdale Boat Show in November of that year. The innovative shoe immediately proved to be popular with children and sporting types in North America and then throughout the world. Wearers enjoy the democratic appeal of Crocs, their bright colours, and what the footwear trade describes as their "ugly" appearance. They would not be out of place in Kmart or Walmart.

In June 2004, the U.S. company bought Foam Creations and acquired the rights to croslite. Here again is an instance of Americans adding design and marketing value to a Canadian invention and thus giving it widespread appeal. It is difficult to find basic information about the pre-Croc: when it launched, who did it, what design, how it was marketed, and so on. In the words of the American company's website, "By 2003 Crocs had become a bona-fide phenomenon, universally accepted as an all-purpose shoe for comfort and fashion."

273. Where will you find the oldest continuously operating, legitimate theatre in North America?

The Royal Alexandra Theatre is considered to be the oldest continuously operating legitimate theatre in North America. As well, it was the first theatre to be fireproofed and then air-conditioned. It is also the sole remaining theatre with a "royal designation" in North America. The exterior of the building is beaux-arts in design; the interior is well described as "a jewel-box."

The Royal Alex was built by the Mulock family of Toronto and opened for road shows on August 26, 1907. It was acquired by the Mirvish family in 1963, which went on to purchase London's Old Vic Theatre and then to construct the nearby Princess of Wales Theatre. It has hosted international touring productions with famous actors and actresses, the annual *Spring Thaw* satires, and the Canadian premiers of such musicals as *Oklahoma*, *Hair*, and *Les Miserables*. It seats 1,500 people, with two balconies.

The Royal Alex has contributed to Toronto's reputation as a "show business city." Indeed, the city itself is often described as the third-largest theatre centre in the English-speaking world (after London and New York), as well as North America's third-largest movie and television production centre (after Los Angeles and Chicago).

274. Is Kraft Cheese a Canadian product?

For three-quarters of a century in North America, the name "Kraft" has identified the leading brand of packaged, processed cheese. The company bears the name of J.L. Kraft, who was born in Fort Erie, Ontario. He revolutionized cheese production and consumption by inventing "process cheese."

At the age of twenty-nine he moved to Buffalo and then Chicago, where he began supplying cheeses to grocers from a horse-drawn wagon. He founded J.L. Kraft & Bros. Company in 1909, and five years later opened his first cheese factory. In 1916 he patented a new cheese pasteurizing process to prevent spoilage and allow cheese to be transported over long distances. The taste of his cheddars was mild rather than sharp, thereby effecting a change in taste preference. The Kraft company was a progressive marketer and promoted brand recognition. In 1933 it began sponsoring *The Kraft Music Hall* and *The Kraft Television Theatre*, popular weekly programs.

So, Kraft Cheese is a North American product that grew from roots in Canada.

275. What is poutine and where did it come from?

Poutine is a French-Canadian dish, high in cholesterol, that consists of French fries with gravy and cheese curds. It has long been popular with working men and for some years it has been considered a Quebec specialty. Sonia Verma is the author of "The Sticky Mess of the Origins of Poutine," which appeared in the *Globe and Mail*, December 7, 2009. Her article focuses on two Quebec communities that claim to have originated this "delicacy."

One account goes that it was originated by Fernand Lachance at his restaurant *Le Lutin Qui Rit* (The Laughing Elf) in Warwick, a town northeast of Montreal. In 1957 a customer asked him to mix fries and cheese curds. Lachance called it a *maudite poutine*, slang for "damned mess." He later added homemade gravy. The town of Warwick established its annual "Poutine Festival" in 1993.

Another account credits Jean-Paul Roy, proprietor of the drive-in restaurant Le Roy Jucep, Drummondville, northeast of Montreal. It seems in 1964 he added cheese curds to his popular *patate-sauce*, or fries and gravy. He listed the item on his menu as a pudding, calling it *Ti-Pout*, or Poutine. His restaurant currently serves nineteen different kinds of poutine. In 2008 the city established its two-day Festival of Poutine.

276. What is Cavena Nuda?

Cavena Nuda is the brand name of a new, unique grain product that resembles rice. It was introduced to the Canadian and world market in 2005 by Scott Sigvaldson of Wedge Farms Nutrition Ltd. His family farm was founded by Jakob Sigvaldason in Arborg, Manitoba, in 1903.

Avena nuda is Latin for "naked oats." With the capital letter C added to indicate Canada, *Cavena Nuda* means "Canadian Naked Oats." It is an oat grain that is "naked" in the sense of being naturally hull-free, unlike rice. With its nutty flavour and a chewy texture, however, it resembles rice. Indeed, it has been described as the "Rice of the Prairies." It is grown only in Manitoba.

As Scott Sigvaldason has explained, "I came across this seed, a new grain developed by Dr. Vern Burrows and Agriculture Canada after decades of research. It was experimental at the time. We grew it quickly and determined it had huge potential beyond pig feed. It is a rice alternative. It looks, cooks and tastes like rice — but it is an oat. It has 2.5 times the protein of rice; it has high beta glucan levels so it lowers the cholesterol and it has a low glycemic index, which means it can be used as part of a diabetic diet."

Cavena Nuda is being marketed to restaurant chefs in the Winnipeg area and is now being supplied to specialty food shops and supermarkets across the country in 1.5-kilogram or 750-gram packages.

277. What are the names of some Canadian delicacies and delights?

Here are the names of some edibles that most Canadians enjoy eating, sometimes exclusively, but not always so. These items rank high in the hierarchy of favourite foodstuffs. Some foods are identified by their familiar brand names; other items bear generic names. All of these delicacies should make your mouth water! How many have you enjoyed?

Arctic Char, Butter Tarts, Canada Dry Ginger Ale, Crispy Crunch Chocolate Bars, Date Squares, Fiddleheads, Icewine, Laura Secord Chocolates, McIntosh Apples, McIntosh Toffee Bars, Maple Syrup, Molson Canadian, Montreal Bagels, Montreal Smoked Meat, Murchie's Teas and Coffees, Nanaimo Bars, Newfie Screech, Pablum, Poutine, President's Choice Products, Quebec Yellow Pea Soup, Red Rose Tea, Rogers' Chocolates of Victoria, Scrunchins, Smarties, Timbits, Tim Hortons Coffee, Winnipeg Golden Eye.

ideas

278. What inscription appears on the monument of Sir Arthur Doughty at the Library and Archives Canada?

The following noble inscription appears on the plinth of the statue of Sir Arthur Doughty, founder of the National Archives of Canada (now Library and Archives Canada) in Ottawa. In 1935, the statue was erected in the building's courtyard.

As Doughty said, "Of all national assets, archives are the most precious; they are the gift of one generation to another and the extent of our care of them marks the extent of our civilization." These are wise words, especially so in our era of instantaneous electronic communication. The sentence is taken from Doughty's book *The Canadian Archives and Its Activities* (1924). Prime ministers and provincial premiers are no strangers to having statues erected in their honour, but the achievements of very few deputy ministers have been so acknowledged. Curiously, the statue of Doughty was so positioned that he is facing Rideau River — and his backside faces the Archives!

279. Which Canadian documents are registered with the Memory of the World Programme?

The Memory of the World Programme was established by UNESCO (United Nations Educational, Scientific and Cultural Organization), which produces a registry designed (in the words of its website) "to preserve and raise awareness of documentary heritage, the memory of the world, which reflects the diversity of languages, peoples and cultures. The programme was born of the realization that this memory is fragile and that important documentary material is lost every day."

UNESCO's International Advisory Committee meets every two years to study nominations by member states. Canada is a member state but has had no international advisors on the committee and no national committee. By 2005 there were twenty-nine collections of documents in the Memory of the World Programme — manuscripts, recordings, films, etc., from twenty-four different countries. Each document is considered to be a work of world significance. For instance, France had three documents: Charles de Gaulle's "Appeal to the French People" broadcast by BBC Radio on June 18, 1950; over 1,000 short films produced by the Lumière brothers; and fonds (a collection of manuscripts) associated with the introduction of the decimal and metric system of measurement. A flurry of activity brought delayed recognition to three Canadian caches of documents, and in 2007 two of them were added to the world registry: the Hudson's Bay Company Archival Records (1670–1920) and the Quebec Seminary Collection (1623–1800). In 2009 Norman McLaren's NFB film *Neighbours* and its associated documents were added. In addition to the international registry, there are over sixty national registries. For instance, the Australian Memory of the World Registry has fifteen entries. Canada has no national committee and hence no national registry.

280. What is "Bambi Meets Godzilla" all about?

Now almost a catchphrase in popular culture, *Bambi Meets Godzilla* is a short animated film about a doe-like deer munching on foliage until, without warning, it is stepped on and squashed by a gigantic, gorilla-like foot. That is all that happens in the black-and-white film, which is 1 minute and 29 seconds in length. According to the amusingly written screen credits, Marv Newland did it all: writer, screenwriter, choreographer, producer, and supervisor of the "wardrobe." As for "production," it was supplied "by Mr. and Mrs. Newland." The credits continue, "We gratefully acknowledge the City of Tokyo for their help in obtaining Godzilla."

The oddly affecting short animated feature was released January 1, 1969. It comprises the talented animator's diploma work for the Los Angeles Center College of Design. The next year, he moved to Toronto; in 1972, he permanently settled in Vancouver, where he established a production studio for animation called International Rocketship, which has distinguished itself in work for commercial houses and the National Film Board.

What is the movie "all about"? It is possible to read a lot into this brief film, but it is essentially a *jeu d'esprit*. One critic suggested the subtext is "Disney meets Darwin," that is, design versus predestination. Quirky TV director David Lynch has produced a spinoff about a car driver who, failing to avoid a deer on the road, crashes his car into the deer but amazingly leaves it unharmed.

On an interesting note, playwright David Mamet titled his acerbic account of the film business *Bambie vs. Godzilla* (2007).

281. How many words do Eskimos have for the word "snow"?

Everyone who knows the answer to that question also knows that Eskimos are now called Inuit. But the answer to and the original question is not 200, 48, 27, or 13, or 9. The answer is quite prosaic, according to linguist Geoffrey Pullum, author of *The Great Eskimo Vocabulary Hoax and other Irreverent Essays on the Study of Language* (Chicago: University of Chicago Press, 1991).

Pullum observes that it is not unreasonable to assume that dwellers in the Far North have a variety of words for the white stuff, no less than printers or graphic designers have different names for fonts of type (Times Roman, Helvetica, Cartier, etc.). Yet, the original inhabitants have perhaps one dozen such words, comparable to such English nouns for specific types of snow as avalanche, blizzard, dusting, hardpack, flurry, hail, sleet, slush, and so on. The urban myth has been traced back to 1911 when anthropologist Franz Boas observed that the Eskimos used four unrelated word roots for snow. Theorists Edward Sapir and Benjamin Lee Whorf inflated the number to seven and the popular press took it from there. Many years ago John MacDonald of the Nunavut Research Institute observed that, however many words there are for snow, Inuktitut has no word for camel.

282. Did Pierre Berton write a preamble to the Canadian Constitution?

There is no preamble to the Canadian Constitution of 1982. However, one was written by Prime Minister Pierre Elliott Trudeau, with the assistance of his advisers, but it inspired no one who read it and so was formally rejected by the provincial premiers.

The *Toronto Star* commissioned a number of distinguished Canadians to compose their own possible preambles. Among the people asked was Pierre Berton, whose prefatory remarks were particularly apt and even witty. The full text of the preamble appeared in the newspaper on April 16, 1982. It goes like this:

> Whereas, we Canadians are the only people in all the Americas to free ourselves non-violently from our European roots;
>
> And, whereas, we have been prepared to wait two centuries to achieve, bloodlessly, what others have seized in a sudden explosion of arms;
>
> And, whereas, this act of gradualism, maddening to some, is at the heart of the Canadian character;
>
> Therefore, we do announce, proclaim, order and establish an all-Canadian constitution, returned to these shores as a symbol of our nonviolent, if somewhat phlegmatic and cautious character,
>
> Together with, a Charter of Rights, expressly designed to provide future employment to the multitudinous graduates of our law schools;
>
> And we do this with humility and quiet pride, having, alone among our neighbours (though with some considerable name calling), managed to achieve our special form of democracy with a minimum of spilled blood.

283. What is remarkable about the portrait of Brian Mulroney in the House of Commons?

By tradition, portraits of retired prime ministers are commissioned by Parliament and then hung on the walls of its halls.

Russian-born artist Igor Babailov was selected to paint the official portrait of Brian Mulroney, and when it was unveiled on November 19, 2002, commentators noted that there is "an inscrutable look" on the former prime minister's face. The phrase is that of columnist Hugh Winsor in "The Power Game," the *Globe and Mail*, November 20, 2002:"He painted Mr. Mulroney with a smile that from some angles turns into a smirk."

The effect is curious, but was it contrived? Was it calculated like Philippe Hébert's life-size statue of Evangeline in Grand Pré National Park, Nova Scotia, which depicts the Acadian heroine as a happy young girl or as a sad older woman, depending on the viewer's vantage point? No one knows....

284. What important events occurred in Canada on September 5, 1945?

Two important events occurred on September 5, 1945. Early that morning, Canada's first successful nuclear reactor became operative at Chalk River, Ontario. Early that evening, Soviet cipher clerk Igor Gouzenko defected from the Soviet Embassy in Ottawa. The first event marked Canada's entry into the atomic age. The second event heralded the advent of the Cold War, characterized by Soviet espionage and U.S. atomic secrecy.

285. Do groundhogs predict the weather?

Rural traditions in North America hold that if a groundhog emerges from its hole on February 2 and fails to find its shadow, it means winter is almost over. If it sees its shadow, it means a long winter lies ahead. In truth, the groundhog does no "seeing"; it is farmers and others observers who act as "seers."

The Canadian media has fixed on two groundhogs: Nova Scotia's Shubenacadie Sam and Ontario's Wiarton Willie. The American equivalent is Pennsylvania's Punxsutawney Phil.

The tradition of having a large rodent forecast the weather goes back about a century. It is said to be based on the Scottish rhyme: "If Candlemas Day is bright and clear, / There'll be two winters in the year." It is said that in the early 1880s, some residents of Punxsutawney, Pennsylvania, decided to celebrate Candlemas Day by going to the woods in search of a groundhog.

Each February, CBC Radio reports on what the groundhogs could "see." As for the reliability of the predictions, CBC News Online noted on February 2, 2002, "There's no hard data on the accuracy of any of their predictions."

286. What is the meaning of the word atanarjuat?

The word *atanarjuat* means "the fast runner" in Inuktitut, the language of the Inuit. The word came to national and international attention with the release of the feature film *Atanarjuat: The Fast Runner*, the world's first feature-length dramatic film written, produced, directed, and acted by the Inuit. It was the first feature to be directed by Zacharias Kunuk. A co-production of Isuma Igloolik and the National Film Board of Canada, it was released for viewing at film festivals in 2001 and for general release in North America in 2002.

It was shot on location on Baffin Island in Nunavut and the dialogue was delivered entirely in Inuktitut (with subtitles). It stars Inuit actor Natar Ungalaaq as Atanarjuat, who falls in love with the lovely Atuat. To win her hand he must run naked through the snow for three days, a custom with traditional meaning. It concerns the rivalry between two runners for Atuat's affections. The theme is the clash between individual desire and community need.

On September 11, 2001, the film was a special presentation at the Toronto International Film Festival. Establishing the commercial and cultural viability of all Inuit cinema, it was followed by two more successful feature films: *The Journals of Knud Rasmussen* (about the interaction of the Inuit and the Danish explorer) in 2006, and *Before Tomorrow* (a period piece about possible starvation in the Arctic) in 2009.

287. What are Father Lonergan's precepts?

Father Bernard J.F. Lonergan (1904–1984) was a member of the Society of Jesus and the leading theologian and philosopher associated with the Roman Catholic Church in Canada. The University of Toronto Press has issued his collected works in a series of more than twenty-six volumes of influential philosophical studies.

Insight: A Study of Human Understanding (1957) offers his "transcendental precepts," or guides as to how one should live his or her life. There are five precepts in all, of which the first precept is the fundamental one. It is "Be attentive." The four precepts that follow are "Be intelligent," "Be reasonable," "Be responsible," and "Be in love."

288. What is UArctic?

UArctic is the nickname of the University of the Arctic, a network of over thirty institutions and organizations of higher education located in the circumpolar regions of the world. These regions include Canada, Alaska, Russia, Finland, Sweden, Norway, Denmark, Greenland, and the Faroe Islands.

UArctic was established on June 12, 2001, with the coordinating office at Rovaniermi, Finland. Its motto is "In the North, for the North, and by the North." It seeks to meet the needs of "Students with Latitude" and offers a Bachelor of Circumpolar Studies. It specializes in Arctic sustainability studies, and meets the needs of Arctic residents through an online learning environment and distance learning.

Among the Canadian institutions involved are Athabasca University (Athabaska, Alberta), Aurora College (Fort Smith, Northwest Territories), Lakehead University (Thunder Bay, Ontario), Nunavut Arctic College (Arviat, Nunavut), University of Alberta (Edmonton, Alberta), University of Northern British Columbia (Prince George, British Columbia), and Yukon College (Whitehorse, Yukon Territory).

289. What is the Canadian connection of the Sara Lee Corporation?

The Sara Lee Corporation is a leading global manufacturer and marketer of brand name consumer packaged goods: packaged meats and bakery, coffee and grocery, household and personal care, and personal products. It is based in Chicago, Illinois, and has manufacturing operations in nearly forty countries. It sells its products in more than 140 countries.

It was formally organized in 1939 as Consolidated Foods and became the Sara Lee Corporation in 1985. Consolidated was founded by Nathan Cummings (1896–1985) and directed by him until his retirement in 1968. Cummings was born in Canada and began his career in his father's shoe store. By 1917 he had built his own shoe manufacturing firm and was gradually expanding it. In 1939 he borrowed $5.2 million to purchase the C.D. Kenny Company (a tea and coffee company) in Baltimore, the first of a series of acquisitions, consolidations, and diversifications. Later, in 1956, he acquired the kitchens of Sara Lee, a five-year-old business producing frozen baked goods. Non-food sales eventually overtook food sales in 1975. Along the road, Sara Lea acquired another company with Canadian connections: Candelle.

Candelle was a Montreal-based lingerie company whose designer Louise Poirier created and named the famous brassiere known as the Wonderbra. Launched in 1964 it consisted of fifty-four design elements that produced the desired "plunge and push effect" to maximize cleavage and minimize the effects of gravity. It sold particularly well in Europe. Sara Lee acquired Candelle in 1991, and on May 9, 1994, it launched the "One and Only Wonderbra" in the United States to great fanfare. In magazine advertisements, supermodel Eva

Herzigova said, while wearing the bra, "Look me in the eyes and tell me that you love me." It made Sara Lee a leader in lingerie throughout the world.

290. Whatever were the so-called Quebec Round and Canada Round?

These were nicknames of two separate initiatives of the second Mulroney administration to secure first ministers' approval for a devolution of federal power to the provinces. The "Quebec Round," called the Meech Lake Accord, was not approved by two provincial legislatures in 1990. The "Canada Round," called the Charlottetown Agreement, concluded in Prince Edward Island's capital on August 28, 1992, was the subject of a country-wide referendum held on October 26, 1992, when it was rejected by voters in British Columbia and Quebec.

291. What is the "Canada clause"?

The inclusion of a so-called Canada clause in the Canadian Constitution was one of the constitutional proposals of the Mulroney administration. This clause was the one titled "Sharing Canada's Future Together," which was tabled in the House of Commons on September 24, 1991. It includes the following sentence: "The Government of Canada proposes that a Canada clause that acknowledges who we are as a people, and who we aspire to be, be entrenched in section 2 of the Constitution Act, 1867."

The document lists some "characteristics and values" of the country and its people: federation; equality of men and women; fairness; aboriginal self-government; bilingualism; Quebec's status as a "distinct society"; multiculturalism; tolerance for individuals, groups, and communities; sustainable environmental development; respect for rights of citizens and communities; free trade within the country; "a commitment to the well-being of all Canadians"; a commitment to the democratic parliamentary system of government; "the balance that is especially Canadian between personal and collective freedom on the one hand and, on the other hand, the personal and collective responsibility that we all share with each other."

292. How does the official Census refer to "language spoken"?

Statistics Canada conducts a mini-census every five years, and it asks residents a series of questions about language. These may be conveniently classed under three headings:

Home Language: "What language does this person speak most often at home?"

Mother Tongue: "What is the language that this person first learned at home in childhood and still understands?"

Knowledge of Languages: "What language(s) can this person speak well enough to conduct a conversation?"

293. What are the summer holidays?

School children love summer holidays — three months free of primary and secondary school. Of adult interest are the three statute holidays that are celebrated within an eleven-day period every summer. These are National Aboriginal Day (June 21), Saint-Jean-Baptiste Day (June 24), and Canada Day (July 1).

National Aboriginal Day was first recognized in 1976, Saint-Jean-Baptiste Day has been a Quebec holiday for decades, and Canada Day (formerly Dominion Day) dates from 1867 and marks the anniversary of Confederation. Interestingly, Canada Day is not the holiday in Quebec that it is in the rest of the country, for it corresponds to "moving day," the day when many residential leases conclude, which results in a shortage of moving vans.

294. What is Flag Day?

Flag Day, first celebrated on February 15, 1996, is dedicated to the Maple Leaf flag, but it isn't a national holiday. It originally celebrated the thirty-first anniversary of an act that recognized the newly created Maple Leaf flag as the national flag of Canada. In an attempt to bolster the spirit of nationalism in the wake of the Quebec referendum, Prime Minister Jean Chrétien promoted Flag Day and attended the first celebration in a park in Hull, Quebec. The occasion was marked by organized heckling and a scuffle between the prime minister and a protester who was representing both the separatists and the unemployed.

295. Did Walt Disney ever control the image of the Mounties?

No. The Mounted Police Foundation was established in 1994 to regulate the commercial use of the RCMP's symbols and image, and the following year it concluded a licensing agreement with Walt Disney Company (Canada) Ltd. to protect and oversee the awarding of licenses. According to Michael Dawson, writing in *The Mountie: From Dime Novel to Disney* (1998), the Force's proportion of royalties was directed to support community policing projects. At the time, there was much public comment on the commercialization of a national icon, its Americanization, and its "Disneyfication" in the hands of Hollywood. Yet, it was nothing more than a licensing arrangement. In any case, the Foundation decided it could continue its licensing itself, so the connection with Disney was ended in 1999.

296. What are the Salmon Arm Salute and the Shawinigan Handshake?

These references are genuine Canadianisms that are sure to bring smiles of recognition to Canadians who recall the 1980s and 1990s.

The Salmon Arm Salute is a jocular reference to "the finger" that Prime Minister Pierre Elliott Trudeau gave to hecklers of his election campaign at Salmon Arm, British Columbia, in the summer of 1983. The Shawinigan Handshake is another facetious reference, this one to Prime Minister Jean Chrétien giving an obstreperous protestor a form of half-nelson in Ottawa on February 16, 1996.

297. What was Operation Fish?

Operation Fish was the code name for shipping Britain's gold and securities to Canada during the Second World War. When the shipments arrived safely, they were deposited in Montreal bank vaults as well as in other cities across the country. They were safeguarded by the RCMP. The full story is told by Alfred Raper in *Operation Fish* (1979). The whole episode sounds like it has the makings of a good movie.

298. Is Victoria Day celebrated in Quebec?

Not by that name in French Canada.

Victoria Day is a statutory holiday celebrated across Canada in all provinces and territories. It marks the birthdays of Queen Victoria and Queen Elizabeth II, and at one time it enjoyed an association with the British Empire. The celebration goes back to 1845; since 1952 it has been observed on the first Monday preceding May 25. The holiday is fondly remembered by school children in English Canada as "the twenty-fourth of May, the Queen's birthday."

Quebec officials have always taken a dim view of Canada's British connection, so in Quebec the holiday was designated *Fête de Dollard-Des-Ormeaux* and it marked the patriotic defence of Montreal by

Adam Dollard in 1666. This did not last. In 2002 the Bloc Québécois changed the *Fête* to *Journée nationale des Patriotes*, or National Patriotes Day, to acknowledge the French rebels who are known as the *Patriotes* of 1837–38.

299. What is the greatest number of goals recorded in a World Championship hockey match?

In the World Championship hockey game played in 1949, Canada defeated Denmark 47–0. This is the most goals ever scored by both teams combined in a game; as well, it is the most goals scored by any one team in a World Championship match, according to the *Guinness Book of World Records* (1975).

300. How long are NHL hockey players on the ice at any one time?

Most hockey fans are surprised to learn that the average hockey player during a National Hockey League game is on the ice for only forty seconds at a time. That at least was the average in 2003. It may be even less today because the duration of the "sprint" has been decreasing with the years. The shift of the average player in 1952 was two minutes. In those days they had endurance; these days they have strength.

The effect of duration on play was noted by Ken Dryden in his article titled "Saving the Game" in the *Globe and Mail*, March 27, 2004: "Playing two minutes at a time, a player has to play a coasting-bursting style of game to save energy. You coast in the neighbourhood of the puck at most moments, then when there is an offensive chance or a defensive urgency, you burst. Playing 40 seconds at a time, you burst all the time. You play at a sprint. I remember little of high school physics, but I do remember: F = ma. Force equals mass times acceleration. So when a body that weighs 29 pounds more moves at a sprinting speed, the force of collision is significantly, dangerously greater."

301. Did a Canadian coin the term "antipsychotics"?

Yes. Credit for coining the term *antipsychotics* has been awarded to Heinz E. Lehmann, psychiatrist at the Verdun Protestant Hospital outside Montreal. Dr. Lehmann is remembered for the introduction of the antipsychotic medication chlorpromazine into the western hemisphere. He published the key scientific paper on its effects in the *Archives of General Psychiatry*, February 1954. Dr. Lehmann introduced the term *antipsychotic* to replace the term *tranquilizer*, shortly after July 1958. First public use of the term occurred at a medical conference in Czechoslovakia. Source: Dr. Thomas A. Ban's "Heinz Lehmann and Psychopharmacology" (unpublished paper, 1999).

302. Were there wartime spies at the NFB?

There were never any spies at the National Film Board of Canada — none during the Second World War, the Cold War, or anytime thereafter.

John Grierson, the documentary filmmaker, served as the Board's first commissioner from 1939 to 1945 and held the rank of deputy minister. About forty years later, a biographer decided Grierson was a Soviet spy and tried to prove the charge, but to no avail. There was no evidence that Grierson or anyone else connected with the Board worked as a spy or a mole. Indeed, the Board produced numerous documentaries about spy networks and the threat of espionage.

Tom Daly, a young film researcher in the 1940s, later a leading executive producer, writing in *How to Make or Not to Make a Canadian Film* (1968), tells an amusing story about a "spy scare" in the early days of the Board, when it still had its headquarters in Ottawa. (It later moved to Montreal.) He discusses stock shots to illustrate his points:

> My job was to find the material that said it visually, or could be stretched or twisted to say it. Only once were we driven to shooting some fake scenes. Absolutely no film material existed of the Haushofer Geopolitical Institute in Munich which we had to talk about. So I shot some scenes in the Film Board offices and corridors to simulate the activities of the Geopolitical Institute. So well known were we for unearthing the real thing that no one suspected this scene. We later got requests from American filmmakers for copies of these "stock shots," and naturally we carried through the charade. We also got a visit from the RCMP who thought we had a German spy. A sharp-eyed American film man in California, who had visited the NFB, had recognized one of the handsome girls in the "Haushofer Institute" as now working for the National Film Board of Canada, and had tipped off the FBI who called the Mounties.

A Californian might think a spy was evidenced; a U.S. senator like Joe McCarthy might try to brand Board members as communist or "communistic sympathizers," but luckily for Canada and for the Board, saner counsel prevailed.

303. Was is the CCPA and how does it affect every Canadian?

The CCPA is the Canadian Centre for Policy Alternatives / Centre canadien de politiques alternatives. It is one of Canada's leading progressive policy research organizations. As such, it resembles the Fraser Institute and the C.D. Howe Institute, conservative or neo-conservative "think tanks," except that the CCPA is progressive and reformist. It was founded in 1980 by academic, labour, and civil society researchers, and it is supported by its more than 10,000 individual and organizational members. Its national headquarters is in Ottawa, with provincial offices in British Columbia, Saskatchewan, Manitoba, and Nova Scotia.

The CCPA affects everyone, because its voice on social policy is heeded in government offices and corporate boardrooms. It produces books, studies, reports, fact sheets, and other publications, including the *CCPA Monitor* and the quarterly *Our Schools / Our Selves*. These publications analyze current issues and offer alternative policy solutions that advance a social and economic justice agenda.

304. What is the Perimeter Institute?

Everything about the Perimeter Institute is big ... gigantic, in fact. Its full name is the Perimeter Institute for Theoretical Physics. It was formally opened in Waterloo, Ontario, on October 23, 2000. This was all made possible with a $100 million donation made by Mike Lazaridis, President of Research in Motion, the developer of the BlackBerry. The institute's endowment is augmented with regular grants from various levels of government.

The purpose of the institute is no less than the study of the nature of the universe. It has an international focus on cutting-edge research in foundational theoretical physics. It offers leading physicists from around the world five-year fellowships to study quantum gravity, string theory, quantum information theory, and the foundations of quantum mechanics. It sponsors seminars, conferences, and organizes public lectures (one of the first was delivered by Sir Roger Penrose). Its physicists — at the time of writing there are nine — have cross-appointments with faculty at the nearby University of Waterloo.

The Perimeter Institute is an independent organization; it is engaged in foundational research (that is, non-directed and basic research), it is resident-based (that is, not dictated by an agenda), it is non-hierarchical in faculty structure, and it is very much concerned with communicating the importance of its research to the public.

Indeed, one of its publications quotes the words of Niels Bohr: "Anyone who has not been shocked by quantum physics has not understood it."

305. How long is *The Fundamentals of Canadian Income Tax?*

Quite long indeed. The eighth edition of *The Fundamentals of Canadian Income Tax*, Vera Krishna's mammoth tome for lawyers and accountants, opens: "Income tax law had a reputation of being a difficult and dry subject. Its reputation for difficulty is justified, but dry or unpleasant it is not."

How long is "quite long indeed"? The pagination goes like this: 92 introductory pages plus 1,752 pages of text, plus 91 pages of index, creating a total of 1,935 pages. Some arithmetic: If there are 500 words or numbers on each page, that means it takes 967,500 words to describe the "fundamentals" of the federal income tax system. And that description covers only the basics of the Income Tax Act. Imagine how many words and numbers it would take to describe all of the details!

306. Were there any years the Stanley Cup was not awarded?

Yes. The Stanley Cup, the oldest trophy in professional sports in North America, was originally donated by Governor General Lord Stanley to encourage competition in hockey. It has been awarded to winning teams every year since the 1892–93 season — with the exception of two seasons.

The games were suspended in for the 1918–19 season at the request of public health officials, who were attempting to restrict the spread of influenza. The Spanish flu epidemic was responsible for the deaths of 50,000 Canadians and 21 million people worldwide over a two-year period.

The season of 2004–05 was formally cancelled on February 16, 2005, in what was known as the "lockout." This lockout of players lasted 154 days. Negotiations between the club owners of the National Hockey League and the players represented by the NHL Players' Association failed to reach a compromise on a maximum team salary cap. Affected were 30 teams, 792 players, 1,230 regular season games, and millions of hockey fans in North America. Cancellation called into question the parlous state of Canada's national game — highly commercialized, given to violent outbreaks, and "professionalized."

As one sports commentator suggested, the Stanley Cup went unawarded the first time because of influenza, the second time because of "affluenza." Ken Dryden, former hockey star, wryly observed, "Canadians will have to decide whether hockey is a habit or a passion."

Indeed, the trustees of the Stanley Cup were encouraged by hockey fans to remove the cup from the control of the National Hockey League and award it, for one year at least, to a non-League team, perhaps a women's hockey team.

307. Is eBay a Canadian success story?

Not really. It has been called "the pioneer of the person-to-person online auction," as since its inception, it has been *the* website for bidding on products and services.

The service was founded in 1995 by Pierre Omidyar, and its first employee and president (regarded as co-founder) is Jeff Skoll, who was born in Montreal in 1965 and raised in Toronto. He is a graduate in electrical engineering from the University of Toronto, and holds an M.B.A. from the Stanford Graduate School of Business. In 2003, *Fortune* listed Skoll as the fourth richest American under forty (the third being Pierre Omidyar), with his personal wealth estimated at US $2.63 billion.

A man with a social conscience, Skoll initially promoted the eBay Foundation; in 1999 he established the Skoll Foundation, based in California'a Silicon Valley, for philanthropy, specifically in support of social entrepreneurs and innovative non-profit organizations working to better communities throughout the world.

While Omidyar has no known Canadian connection, it is interesting that the name of eBay brings to mind — to Canadian minds, at least — the "The Bay," the trading name of the Hudson's Bay Company. The HBC, founded in 1670, was considered to be the world's oldest incorporated joint-stock merchandising company, at least until the 1990s when the corporate enterprise collapsed. Around the same time, eBay came into existence. The "Bay" of eBay is not the HBC, but the Bay area of San Francisco, the location of its corporate headquarters.

308. Is it an urban legend that the Tim Hortons outlets spike their coffee with nicotine?

Yes, it is a legend. No, the Tim Hortons chain of coffee shops does not add nicotine to their coffee, donuts, or other baked goods.

Tim Hortons is the country's best-known chain of outlets for coffee and fresh-baked goods. "Always Fresh" is the company's slogan. The outlets are "always open." The chain was founded in 1964 and has more than 2,000 outlets across Canada as well as many locations in the United States. Its coffee is described as a "special blend" and the specific ingredients and preparation processes are a company-held secret.

The popularity of the coffee probably generated the rumours that its products were addictive and that the ingredient responsible was nicotine. Why nicotine? It is highly toxic, even in small amounts, and is not permitted to be used as a food additive in either Canada or the United States.

No evidence of nicotine was ever found in the chain's coffee or baked goods. The amount of caffeine in the coffee is about the same as in Starbucks or Second Cup brews. The urban legend was the subject of CBCTV's *Disclosure* telecast in February 2004.

309. What is DART?

The Canadian Armed Forces authorized the formation of the Disaster Assistance Response Team in the 1990s. Popularly known as DART, it consists of a team of military personnel, including soldiers, doctors, and engineers, who are especially trained in emergency relief operations. DART's home base is CFB Trenton, Ontario, and its response time is forty-eight hours. DART has responded to the Honduras hurricane (1998), the Turkey earthquake (1999), and Sri Lanka (2004–05). The last major mission was in response to the undersea earthquake in December 2004, which produced the Asian tsunami and resulted in the deaths of more than 100,000 people from the littorals of more than a dozen Asian countries.

310. What does it mean that Canada is "the home of the 0.7"?

Canada should devote 0.7 percent of its Gross Domestic Product (GDP) to foreign aid. This was the principal recommendation of a report commissioned by Prime Minister Lester B. Pearson in the 1960s. By 2000 the United Nations had adopted that figure as the target level of aid to be provided for underdeveloped countries from all industrialized countries.

While Canada's levels of spending had risen in the intervening years, by 2005 they had reached only 0.28 percent of GDP. Five countries — Denmark, Norway, Sweden, Netherlands, and Luxembourg — did reach that level, and still other countries (Britain, France, Belgium, Spain, Ireland, and Finland) were committed to doing so. By comparison, the United States devoted only about 0.15 percent of its GDP to development aid.

Canada was urged to meet its goal by the Columbia University economist Jeffrey Sachs. Issuing his own UN-sponsored report, he said, "Canada should have been No. 1. It is the home of the 0.7." Source: Marcus Gee and Estanislao Oziewicz, "Rich Countries Must Boost Aid, Report Says," the *Globe and Mail*, January 18, 2005.

311. Is there a federal department called "The Department of Foreign Affairs and International Trade"?

No, but there once was such a department. A long time ago, and for a long period of time, a department of the federal government was known as the Department of External Affairs. Later, it became the Department of Foreign Affairs. That lasted until 1982, when the department was expanded to cover not only foreign affairs but also international trade relations. For that reason it was christened the Department of Foreign Affairs and International Trade Canada, or DFAIT in short. In 2005 the two wings of the department were separated, so to speak, so that there is now both a Department of Foreign Affairs and a Department of International Trade. The issue was considered by Robert Johnstone in "'Fixing' Foreign Affairs is Flawed," the *Globe and Mail*, January 19, 2005.

312. What is the meaning of *Haida Gwaii*?

Haida Gwaii is the aboriginal name of the Queen Charlotte Islands, the ancestral home of the Haida people. The islands, which cluster along the coast of central British Columbia, are famous for their awesome natural beauty (mountains, tall stands of trees, rainforests, eagles, ravens) and fabled for their human artifacts, which include stands of totem poles and other remnants of Haida settlements.

313. What was the School on Wheels?

In Canada, children being raised in isolated communities along railway lines in Northern Ontario were well served by the School on Wheels. The service was launched by the Canadian Pacific Railway Company on September 20, 1926, when a dedicated teacher named Fred Sloman, accompanied by his wife Cela and their young children, opened the first "schoolcar" on the CP siding at Nandair, northwest of Sudbury. The first pupils and students ranged in age from five to eighteen, and had never before attended a regular school. Some of them even spoke little or no English. They were attracted to the green-painted passenger car, the interior of which had been renovated to provide cramped but adequate living quarters for the Sloman family as well as a classroom with seats for as many as one dozen students. There was also a library of 300 books, including maps and atlases.

The schoolcar would remain on the siding for three to five days and then be hauled to the next isolated community, eventually returning again in a week or so. The School on Wheels proved so popular with children and families that other railways followed suit. Canadian Pacific and Temiskaming and Northern Ontario Railroad also offered versions of the "schoolcar" service along their lines. At any one time, there were as many as five schoolcars on the rails. Over the years, School on Wheels service employed one dozen teachers, before the service was discontinued in 1967.

Fred Sloman himself taught for thirty-nine of those forty-one years. Upon his death, his widow Cela settled in Clinton, Ontario. When she was informed that the original *Schoolcar No. 15089* was headed for the scrap-heap, she led the townfolk to purchase it, outfit it, and transport it to Clinton. There it became the centrepiece of Sloman Memorial Park, and there it may be visited to this day.

314. Does the CBC have a lobby group?

The Canadian Broadcasting Corporation is a Crown corporation and as such does not formally lobby the federal government for additional subsidies or privileges (as might such industries as automotive, pharmacology, insurance, construction, etc.) As well, its operation is regulated by the Canadian Radio-Television and Telecommunications Commission (CRTC). However, to the extent that the CBC represents national broadcasting as opposed to private broadcasting, it is given an assist by the Friends of Canadian Broadcasting, a voluntary association of concerned Canadians. Formed in 1985, the Friends of Canadian Broadcasting (as their literature says) "understand the essential role that the CBC plays in nurturing a distinct political and social culture in Canada. The CBC is the only national institution that speaks to all Canadians, in all regions of the country — making it possible to speak to one another, freely and openly." The Friends of Canadian Broadcasting prepares submissions related to the broadcasting system, and it appears before parliamentary committees and CRTC hearings to present the case for more and better Canadian content. It is more a pressure group than a lobby group.

315. Could the Stanley Cup ever be awarded to a non-NHL team?

As things stand, the answer is "no." Only hockey teams that are members of the National Hockey League may compete for the Stanley Cup. The famous silver bowl, donated by Governor General Lord Stanley in 1893 as a "challenge cup" to be awarded on an annual basis to the winning hockey team, has become identified with professional hockey — that is, commercial hockey — although, in the early days, all the competing teams were amateur teams, there being no commercially organized hockey tournaments at the time.

The Stanley Cup has come to represent professional hockey supremacy, the Allan Cup recognizes supremacy in senior hockey, and the Memorial Cup is for junior hockey. Women's hockey lacked a ceremonial cup or similar award for some time.

Over time, the Stanley Cup came to be identified with the NHL. "The Stanley Cup has been awarded exclusively to the NHL playoff champion every year since 1926," noted Eric Duhatschek in "Stanley Cup Can Only Go to NHL Teams, Trustee Says," the *Globe and Mail*, February 22, 2005.

The fate of the Stanley Cup rests in the hands of its two legally empowered trustees, but their hands have been tied since 1947, when the trustees of the day formalized an agreement with the NHL that the League had "full authority to determine the conditions of competition for the Stanley Cup." That agreement continues to the present day.

If the NHL decides not to hold playoff games and not award the cup any season, no other group is empowered to award it. The cancellation of the season of 2004–05 raised hopes that the cup might be offered on a goodwill basis to recognize supremacy in women's hockey — a movement led by Governor General Adrienne Clarkson. Nothing came of that initiative, but since 2009 the Clarkson Cup has been annually awarded to the winner of the National Canadian Women's Hockey Championship. The trophy was named in honour of former Governor General Adrienne Clarkson.

316. What is the CCCE?

The initials CCCE stand for the Canadian Council of Chief Executives. This is the new name for the old Business Council on National Issues (BCNI), created by lawyer Thomas d'Aquino.

"The CCCE is the country's strongest political lobby," explained Tony Clarke in "National Insecurity," *The CCPA Monitor*, February 2005. "It consists of the top executives of Canada's largest 150 corporations." The executives, as a group, lobbied for the Free Trade Agreement and the North American Free Trade Agreement. Its members favour a corporatist, continentalist approach to economic and political matters. In April 2003 the CCCE unveiled its policy titled the North American Security and Prosperity Initiative, which seeks to reconcile cross-border trade and cross-border security concerns on a North American basis.

317. What are ringette and floor hockey?

Ringette and floor hockey are popular, non-commercial, non-contact, fast-moving team sports.

Both ringette and floor hockey are modelled on ice hockey and were developed by Sam Jacks (1915–1975), parks and recreational director of North Bay, Ontario. Recognizing the fact that hockey has an appeal to youngsters and women as well as to boys and men, he devised these two team games. They are now so popular that there are national and international leagues. They are played by amateurs in many countries of the world.

Jacks developed floor hockey as early as 1936, but it was only in 1970 that it caught on in a big way. It is played by two teams of six players on a surface of wood or concrete instead of ice. There are no skates, sticks, or pucks. Instead, players wear sneakers, wield wooden poles, and drive open-centred disks. Floor hockey is the only team game recognized by the Special Olympics. It was first played on this level at the 1970 Special Olympics Winter Games.

Ringette, sometimes described as "the little sister to hockey," is played on skates and on ice. Like floor hockey, there are two teams, each with six players (one goalie, two defence, one centre, two forwards). A straight stick is used instead of a hockey stuck, and in place of a puck a rubber ring is used. The game is organized on skill levels: Bunnies (learning to skate), C, B, A, AA, and AAA. There are local, regional, national, and international tournaments.

Both ringette and floor hockey are fast-moving games with many players and fans. Competition and cooperation are required in successful play. It has two features that render it superior to hockey: no physical contact between players is allowed, and there is no professional (that is, commercial) element.

318. Who or what is the world's largest purchaser of alcoholic beverages?

The Liquor Control Board of Ontario (LCBO) is often described as the world's largest purchaser of alcoholic beverages (what it inelegantly terms "beverage alcohol"). A monopoly run by the Province of Ontario, the LCBO has immense national and international purchasing power. As of April 2005, the LCBO operated 601 retail stories from five regional warehouses, and it stocks and sells 4,200 quality wines, beers, and coolers. It introduces 3,000 new vintage products each year. Even so, LCBO services only half the province's "beverage alcohol" market, because the other half being is served by 431 beer stores, 364 winery retail stores, 36 brewery retail stores, 11 duty-free stores, 3 distillery stores, plus private ordering. Each year, the LCBO pays a $1.04 billion dividend to the Ontario treasury, plus applicable taxes. Its motto is "LCBO Discover the World."

319. Who consults the *CPS?*

CPS is familiar to every physician and pharmacist in the country and to countless other people employed in the health-care field. The *CPS* is a standard reference work. The initials stand for *Compendium of Pharmaceuticals and Specialties: The Canadian Drug Reference for Health Professionals.* The Canadian Pharmacists Association has released annual volumes in English and French since 1965. The 2005 English edition, the 40th edition, comes as a hefty, blue-covered paperback volume, large in format (9" x 12"), with over 2,000 triple-columned pages of small type, illustrations, charts, and advertisements for current medications. The text is also available on CD-ROM and online. It advertises its service as "Credible Current Canadian."

In its pages, physicians and pharmacists are to find the latest information on available prescription drugs, clinical information, product monographs, therapeutic guides, directories of companies and services, as well as photographs of products for identification purposes. It is not meant for the layperson, but any layperson with an interest in medications and how they are administered would benefit from consulting it in a clinic, pharmacy, or public library.

320. What are the national sports of Canada?

On May 12, 1994, the Parliament of Canada declared ice hockey to be the national winter sport and lacrosse to be the national summer sport. This represents a compromise between present popularity and past prominence. Hockey is widely recognized as "the national sport" but at one time, until the early twentieth century, it was lacrosse that was the favoured game for "gentleman and players."

321. How does the official Acadian flag differ from France's Tricolour?

The official flag of the Acadian people of Nova Scotia, New Brunswick, and Prince Edward Island, adopted in 1884, consists of the National Flag of France plus a yellow star. The French flag, known as the Tricolour, has three panels (blue, white, and red); the Acadian flag has the same three panels, plus a five-pointed yellow star in the blue panel. So the two flags are identical, except for the star.

322. What are the three — some say four — Fs of early Canadian history?

It has been said that the three Fs of early Canadian history are Fish, Fur, and Forests. Indeed, much of the development of the country turned on the exploitation of the fisheries, the fur-trade, and the forestry business.

There is a fourth F. It stands for Faith (that is, Christianity with its emphasis on "spreading the Gospel") — another motive for the exploration, occupation, and cultivation of the land.

323. Who is *The Spirit of Canada*?

A statue of a grieving woman stands alone and in solitude on the dias of the Canadian National Vimy Memorial on the Douai Plain of Northern France. That statue is known as *The Spirit of Canada*. The woman is mourning for the men who fell there. The cloaked figure of the young woman was modelled in London in the Maida Vale studio of Walter S. Allward, the Canadian sculptor and designer of the impressive memorial — the stone carving itself was executed in France. It is said that Allward's model was a young Englishwoman named Edna Jennings (*née* Moynihan). The memorial was dedicated on July 26, 1936. She was not invited to it and never saw the statue that she inspired.

324. Was the referendum on Newfoundland's union with Canada rigged?

Newfoundlanders voted twice on whether or not they wanted to confederate with Canada. In the first referendum, held on June 3, 1948, a total of 155,677 Newfoundlanders voted for Commission Government (14 percent), Confederation with Canada (41 percent), or Responsible Government (45 percent). In the second referendum, held on July 22 of that year, a total of only 149,657 Newfoundlanders voted for Confederation with Canada (52 percent) or Responsible Government (48 percent).

Why were 6,020 fewer votes cast in the second referendum than in the first? Was there a conspiracy to suppress ballots? Harold Horwood, no believer in the conspiracy theory, wrote in his biography *Joey* (1989):

> One or two writers have even published the wild suggestion that the second referendum was fraudulent, and that seven thousand votes for responsible government were destroyed, all as part of the official conspiracy — this fraud being carried out, somehow or other, under the noses of scrutineers from the various responsible government parties, who sat in all the polling booths.
>
> Such speculations could only have been made by people who knew nothing about the social realities of Newfoundland in 1948. On June 3, when the first referendum was held, nearly everyone was at home. On July 22, when the second referendum was held, almost ten thousand fishermen were at least, and only a minority of them managed to reach a polling both. Few of the Labrador floaters (as distinct from the stationers) and few of the banking crews had the chance to a vote at all. Had they been able to reach polling booths, the confederate majority would have been increased accordingly.

The main conspiracy theorist here is Bren Walsh, newspaperman and the author of *More than a Majority: The Story of Newfoundland's Confederation with Canada* (1985). It was Walsh's thesis that the results of the referendum on Confederation were rigged, the majority of Newfoundlanders having voted against Confederation. Walsh added, "That's a supposition concerning which this book, if it does nothing else, certainly raises reasonable doubts." The theory has given birth to a lively movie called *Secret Nation* (1992), which stars Cathy Jones, Mary Walsh, Rick Mercer, and other talented actors who live out the conspiracy. Is it fiction disguised as documentary — or documentary disguised as fiction?

325. Is there a distinctive Canadian speech?

Our Americans cousins are forever assuring us that we speak "with an accent." When pressed, Americans will mention the way Canadians pronounce the first and third words in the expression "out and about." They think we say "oot and aboot." You explain it!

We feel there are two things distinctive about our speech patterns. We tend to append *eh?* at the end of a sentences, and we pronounce the last word of the alphabet as *zed* rather than *zee*.

Some Americans use *eh?* in this way, but none of them pronounce the twenty-sixth letter of the alphabet to rhyme with *bed*.

The Canadian Oxford Dictionary defines *eh* as an "informal interjection," one that may "invite assent" or "ascertain comprehension.": "This is the only usage of *eh* that can be categorized as peculiarly Canadian," the editors explain, "all other uses being common amongst speakers in other Commonwealth countries and to a lesser extent in the United States." Other usages include expressing surprise and asking for a repetition or an explanation.

The British and Canadian pronunciation of the letter *z* as *zed* is derived through the French *zède*, from the Greek *Zeta*.

326. How many of the world's largest banks are Canadian?

In a list of 46 banks of the world, not one is Canadian. Ten are located in the United States, five are based in Japan, another five are situated in the United Kingdom, and four were established in China. The rest of the banks are domiciled in Europe.

327. Where are the world's biggest stock exchanges?

The five biggest stock exchanges in the world (based on capitalization) are those in the United States, Japan, United Kingdom, France, Germany, and Canada, in that order.

328. What are some nicknames for the BlackBerry?

Since the use of the device — including "thumb typing" — is popularly considered to be addictive, like crack, it was quickly dubbed the "CrackBerry." The question "Does it work well?" is answered by "It's all thumbs." Women who find the men in their lives preoccupied with sending and receiving messages, instead of more marital concerns, dubbed it the "BlackWidow." A later, blue-coloured model was nicknamed the "BlueBerry."

329. What is the Ballard fuel cell?

A possible replacement for the internal combustion engine used in automobiles, the Ballard fuel cell is an electrochemical device that combines oxygen with hydrogen to generate electricity, leaving a stream of pure water vapour and heat as its only emissions. Developed in the 1970s by the Ballard Power Systems Inc. of North Vancouver, it was publicly tested in 1993. It bears the name of its inventor Geoffrey Ballard, who was born in Niagara Falls, Ontario, and earned a doctorate in geophysics from Washington University, St. Louis, Missouri. Ballard is an enthusiast for the "hydrogen economy," according to Brian Bergman in "It's Cleanup Time," *Maclean's Special Commemorate Issue 100*, October 2004. With fuel costs soaring, its future might well be assured.

330. What do Canadians have to do with screws?

Canadians invented the heads of two popular screwdrivers. In 1908, Peter Robertson of Milton, Ontario, patented the square-headed driver and screw system. It is superior to the slot-headed driver and screw because the driver, when turned, is less able to slip and "strip" the screw. In 1965 George H. Cluthe, of Waterloo, Ontario, patented "the interchangeable-head screwdriver, with the top handle that swivels open to reveal a variety of bits," explained Barbara Wickens, writing in "Immersed in Canadiana," *Maclean's Special Commemorate Issue 100*, October 2004.

331. What is the Fox 40?

Fox 40 is the brand name of the referee's whistle now sanctioned for use by all major sporting organizations. It was designed by Ron Foxcroft in 1987, who now manufactures it through Fox 40 International.

"Fox" stands for Foxcroft and "40" reflects that the designer/ manufacturer was in his fortieth year when he developed the plastic whistle. Foxcroft, a native of Hamilton, Ontario, and an enthusiastic sportsman, served as a basketball referee at McMaster University. He noted that the regulation "pea whistle," used to referee most sporting events, was unreliable. For instance, it jammed when blown too hard; the "pea" lodged and the whistle failed to sound. Working with a series of prototypes, he evolved a plastic, "pea-less whistle," and its practicality and reliability were immediately recognized by sporting officials.

In addition to running Fox 40 international, Foxcroft served as president of Fluke Transport & Warehousing. The well-known trucking firm's motto is amusing: "If it arrives on time, it's a Fluke."

332. What is the most memorable of all D-Day images?

These are the words of military historian John Keegan:

> The Queen's Own Rifles of Canada was to leave, entirely through the hazard of war, one of the most memorable of all D-Day images. Inside one of its landing craft was a film cameraman, Sergeant Bill Grant. There were several other photographers with the assault troops, but all lost their equipment in the frenzy of the approach. Grant did not, set his camera rolling, and so caught the drama of touchdown and beach crossing. So the viewer sees the infantrymen readying themselves in the last seconds of the run-in — one pats the man ahead of him on the back to receive a "don't bother me now" glance — the ramp goes down, the seawall and beachfront houses appear, and then the riflemen spring down the ramp, cross the sand, into the defenders' fire. The footage is one of the most graphic depictions of combat ever recorded.

Keegan contributed the foreword to *Juno: Canadians at D-Day, June 6, 1944* (2004) by Ted Barris. At the rear of one of the first assault landing crafts of the Queen's Own stood Sergeant William Grant, a member of No. 2 Canadian Film and Photo Unit within the army's Public Relations Unit, who operated a tripod-mounted, hand-wound 35 mm movie camera. Aboard the craft and then on the sand dunes before Bernières-sur-Mer, he shot three hundred feet of black-and-white film. The three reels of undeveloped film were flown to the

Ministry of Information in London. The footage was developed, previewed by censors (who removed frames that showed then-secret British weaponry), edited down to ten minutes, and then released as newsreels to movie theatres.

333. How many Canadian businesses rank in the world's top forty-four largest?

None in 2010. The world's five biggest businesses, based on sales, are (in decreasing order) Walmart Stores, British Petroleum, Exxon Mobil, Royal Dutch/Shell Group, and General Motors. Canada boasts no companies in the major league. Out of the forty-four, the United States has nineteen, Japan eight, Germany four, France four, and the United Kingdom three. The rest are based in the Netherlands, Italy, and Switzerland.

334. Which university has more students studying mathematics than any other?

"The University of Waterloo has the largest engineering enrollment in Canada and the largest mathematical enrollment in the world," noted the business executive Harry T. Seymour in his introduction to an address by Douglas T. Wright, dean of Engineering and then president of the University of Waterloo. Dr. Wright's address, titled "Technology and the Competitive Challenge," was delivered on November 28, 1985, to the Toronto audience of the Empire Club of Canada.

The growth and the importance of the University of Waterloo have been phenomenal. The university was formed in 1957 following the amalgamation of a number of small arts colleges in the "twin cities" of Kitchener and Waterloo. Under the visionary leadership of Dr. Wright, the new university developed strong departments of engineering, mathematics, computers, technology, and science. In tandem it devised its then-unique cooperative program of apprenticeship and placement, which became the model for many other post-secondary institutions of learning.

Waterloo's innovative approach (now accepted as commonplace) certainly influenced the Department of Medicine at McMaster University in nearby Hamilton, Ontario. It also had an effect on the departments of animation and computer-assisted design at the Sheridan Institute of Technology and Advanced Learning, one of Canada's premier polytechnic institutes. Sheridan is located in Oakville and Brampton, Ontario, not far from Hamilton and Waterloo.

Dr. Wright has had this to say about the learning and apprenticeship program: "My experiences at Waterloo with the co-operative program in which study and work experience were closely integrated in a kind of progressive internship suggested to me the value of this kind of process as much for facilitating social adjustments as for training. Most evidence suggests that programs of study are tending to lengthen for a variety of reasons which may be broadly categorized as reflecting a general view that more is better." Source: Douglas T. Wright, "Higher Education in Ontario," Toronto, The Empire Club of Canada, March 16, 1970.

335. Do Canadian newspapers favour American or Canadian spelling?

They favour Canadian spelling now, after a wave of nationalism overtook the editors of Canadian newspapers. It began in October 1990 when the publisher of the *Globe and Mail* changed its paper's long-standing policy on spelling, opting to spell words in the British rather than the American style. The *Toronto Star* did the same in September 1997, and the Southam newspaper chain followed suit in September 1998. The new style is a mixture of British and American — a unique and practical Canadian blend. The stylistic change brings it in line with the official government style introduced by the federal government more than half a century ago.

Up to that time, newspapers and periodicals followed American spelling styles. That made sense, as most newspapers published in this country subscribed to American wire services which favoured "favor" over "favour," "center" over "centre," etc. In a sense the Canadian editors were "coming home," because the earliest newspapers issued in pre-Confederation times followed British styles. American styles were adopted with the advent of wire services.

Associated Press, the U.S. news service, opened its first "foreign" bureau in Halifax in 1849 to cover news of vessels arriving from Europe prior to landing in New York. The Canadian Press news service, established in 1917, opted for AP's spelling until 1998, when CP fell in line with nationalistic sentiments led by "Canada's National Newspaper." Consistency is important and leads to clarity of expression.

Only in the 1980s did English-Canadian newspaper copyeditors begin to add the correct accents to French proper names; for too long, René Lévesque and Jean Chrétien appeared shorn of their accents.

336. Is the "Toronto Brace" shown on an Australian stamp?

As unlikely as it might seem, what is called the "Toronto Brace" is depicted on a postage stamp issued by Australian Post in 1972. The 24-cent stamp was issued on August 2, 1972, in the "Rehabilitation" series, and it shows a nine-year-old boy bouncing a football or soccer ball despite the fact that his legs are supported by a mechanical device. At the time, the youngster was a patient in a rehabilitation centre in New South Wales.

The stamp was issued "to draw attention to the work of various organizations assisting in the rehabilitation of physically and mentally disabled people. It shows a boy in a Toronto split, which, as its name indicates, was designed by a Canadian orthopaedist. The boy shown was afflicted with Perthes syndrome — a disability of the hip. He spent four months in bed in a plaster cast, to position the hip joint correctly, after which the plaster was exchanged for the splint. The steel appliance, padded with leather, is hinged so that the wearer can flex his knees, and move about relatively easily, with the aid of crutches. As the stamp shows, the splint permits child patients to take part in games.

The splint was removed in June, and the boy was able to return home with only a slight limp."

This description comes from the *Australian Post Office Philatelic Bulletin*, September 1972, courtesy of Richard Breckon, historian, Philatelic Group, Australia Post HQ, Melbourne. The device was the inspiration of the Toronto-born orthopaedic surgeon Walter Bobechko (1932–2007) of Toronto's Hospital for Sick Children. The so-called Toronto Brace, designed to free children with Legg-Perthes Orthosis from spending years in leg casts, was developed by Dr. Bobechko in 1968 and is used around the world.

The Australians beat the Canadians in honouring this device on a postage stamp.

337. What is the Montreal procedure?

The most distinguished Canadian of his day was Wilder Penfield (1891–1976). He was regarded as one of the world's leading surgeons and teachers, perhaps second in influence only to Sir William Osler, another Canadian associated with McGill University in Montreal, who set standards in medical procedure and practice.

Dr. Penfield was born in the United States but he settled in Montreal in 1928, where he joined the medical faculty of McGill University. In 1934 he founded the Montreal Neurological Institute, which attained worldwide fame for conducting innovative research and promoting advanced surgical procedures.

The so-called Montreal Procedure, chief among these advanced procedures, called for the surgical excision of parts of the brain afflicted with epilepsy. The operation was conducted on the patient's exposed brain, using local rather than general anaesthesia, with the patient conscious and asked to identify sensory or motor responses as each area of the brain was probed in turn.

With such knowledge, Dr. Penfield and his associates were able to map much of the brain and isolate individual areas responsible for specific motor and sensory responses. This marked not only possible relief for sufferers of epilepsy, but it offered immense possibilities for neurologists and neurosurgeons to understand the human brain and how its form is related to its function.

Dr. Penfield and his associates developed the so-called "Motor and Sensory Homunculus," a series of schematic drawings of a naked human with human features exaggerated in proportion to the density of nerve endings. Thus, for instance, the head and thumb are prominent, whereas the trunk and legs are almost shrunken.

338. What are Northrop Frye's "three Ls"?

The great literary theorist and critic Northrop Frye (1912–1991) taught at Victoria College, University of Toronto, for most of his life. He published a series of important and influential literary studies, including *Fearful Symmetry*, *Anatomy of Criticism*, *The Great Code*, and *Words of Power*. Despite his pre-eminence as a theorist and critic, he often said he saw himself not so much as a scholar but as a teacher. He even described his books as teaching manuals that would be of use to other teachers. Frye was not given to catch-words or catchy formulations, but associated with him and his work are the three Ls: Literacy, the ability to read; Language, the mother tongue and the key to communication and self-knowledge; and Literature, the words used in poetry and fiction to give expression to profound feelings. The notion of the three Ls has not been found in any single passage in any of his writings, but his concern with literacy, language, and literature pervades all of his writing and teaching.

339. What are some words of Canadian origin?

Lexicographers are quite able to compile lists of words of Canadian origin, and quiz masters are quite willing to ask contestants or candidates to spell them and explain their meanings. Such words even turn up in spelling bees, like the national contest called "Can West Can Spell." From its 2007 contest, here is a list of thirty-five Canadianisms, distinctive words that are to be found in *Webster's Third New International Dictionary, Unabridged* (2002):

Albertosaurus

anglophone

atigi

ballicatter

bedlamer

brewis

canol

caribou

cheechako

coulee

dépanneur

frazil

garburator

hackmatack

hoser

Inuktitut

kokanee

labradorite

mucky-muck

muskellunge

Ogopogo

poutine

provincehood

ptarmigan

Qallunaaq

ringette

siwash

skookum

snye

switchel

tricot

triticate

tyee

voyageur

wanigan.

It is unlikely that many Canadians will be able to define all of these Canadianisms, yet individually they may be said to identify aspects of life that are important to specific groups of Canadians. An instance is Inuktitut, the proper name for the language spoken by the Inuit.

340. What are some (more) Canadian connections with *Star Trek*?

The NBC television series *Star Trek* is rich in Canadian connections. Here are a number of passing references (with the episode's title):

- An area free of Borg activity is dubbed "the Northwest Passage." (*Voyager,* "Scorpion Part I")

- A "runabout" ship is dubbed the *Yukon*. (*Deep Space Nine*, "By Inferno's Light")

- Riker is believed to be a Canadian but actually comes from Alaska. (*The Next Generation*, "Lower Decks")

- Counselor Troi consults the *Manitoba Journal of Interplanetary Psychology*. (*The Next Generation*, "The Price")

- The Iconian gateway leads to the New Toronto City Hall. (*The Next Generation*, "Contagion")

- Mr. Spock explains the root grain for the special wheat, identified as quadrotriticale, originated in Canada. (Original series, "The Trouble with Tribbles")

In addition, more than twenty Canadian actors have been featured in the various series:

William Shatner (Captain Kirk)

James Doohan (Scotty)

John Colicos (Kor)

Christopher Plummer (General Chang)

Kim Cattrall (Lieutenant Valeris)

Saul Rubinek (Kivas Fajoy)

Alan Scarfe (Admiral Mendak, Tokath)

Matt Frewer (Rasmussen)

Linda Thorson (Gul Ocett)

Andrea Martin (Ishka)

Geneviève Bujold (Captain Janeway)

Angela Dohrmann (Ricky).

341. What is Canada's contribution to the martial arts?

The contribution is known as Taoist Tai Chi — a form of the traditional Tai Chi Chuan as developed by the Daoist monk Moy Lin-shin (1931–1998), who started teaching first in Montreal and then in Toronto. An immigrant from Hong Kong, he modified the orthodox Yang style Tai Chi Chuan form, integrating it with his knowledge of Lok Hup Ba Fa and other internal rather than martial arts. The new form is designed with health benefits in mind, not defence or meditative practice. Master Moy emphasized the health benefits of Tai Chi and also the spiritual, yet he described it as "meditation in motion."

Toronto is the headquarters of the International Taoist Tai Chi Society, a registered charity, and there are currently 500 branches in more than twenty-six countries. Trained members — membership is open to the public — regularly contribute volunteer service to the community at large. Practitioners learn basic exercises before the more-complicated, mentally and physically challenging set of 108 integrated movements. The set takes about fifteen weeks to learn and about fifteen minutes to execute.

The Fung Loy Kok Institute of Taoism opened on a picturesque, one-hundred-acre tract of land east of Orangeville, Ontario. The structures include a 450-square-metre temple (dedicated to three religious paths: Daoism, Confucianism, Buddhism), a memorial hall, three residential pavilions, fifty-six meditation rooms, as well as a practice hall. The practice hall permits one thousand people to practice at the same time and is believed to be the world's largest designed-and-designated Tai Chi pavilion.

From the society's aims and objectives: "The Fung Loy Kok Institute of Taoism observes the integrated teachings of the three religions of China — Confucianism, Buddhism and Taoism. Its objective is to deliver all from suffering, both the living and the dead, through community service, rituals and ceremonies, and the cultivation of body and mind."

342. What is the "100-day war"?

Never heard of the "100-day war"?

According to commentator Diane Francis, in *Who Owns Canada Now: Old Money, New Money and the Future of Canadian Business* (2008), "That's a term used by developers and contractors and people in the construction trades to refer to the unique ability of Canadian contractors to erect buildings in record time because of the country's short warm-weather season." She goes on to quote developer Lawrence "Larry" Tanenbaum as saying, "Canadians are incredibly efficient at construction because we work in difficult elements. The 100-day war starts the minute frost disappears and we have to get at it. Also, it's a war because the longer construction takes, the more capital costs go up. This means that building here is more expensive unless you work quickly. The result is, the weather and costs have made us more efficient out of sheer necessity." Tanenbaum further noted that this challenge has resulted in Canadian companies being among the world's foremost building, construction, and development contractors.

343. What is PICASSO?

PICASSO brings to the mind the great painter Pablo Picasso. But to physicists and astrophysicists, the letters of that name stand for "Project in CAnada to Search for Supersymmetric Objects." The project is described as "a dark matter search experiment," and this experimental and theoretical work is being undertaken at the SNOLAB (Sudbury Neutrino Observatory), a surface and subsurface laboratory .

The subsurface faculty is located two kilometres underground in INCO's abandoned Creighton mine, near Sudbury, Ontario. SNOLAB's work concentrates on astroparticle physics, studying properties of neutrinos, characteristics of the Sun, and features of dark matter. The PICASSO project is the search for dark matter, which is conjectured to account for 85 percent of all matter in the universe. Astronomers know only the luminous 15 percent.

So, astrophysicists are searing for the hypothetical "weakly inter-active massive particle" known as the "neutralino," which is theorized to be abundant in the universe, but is yet to be directly observed. Officials at PICASSO wrote, "We observe presently an increasing synergy and complementarity between astronomical observations, direct and indirect searches and experiments at accelerators, which makes this field of research one of the most fascinating in contemporary science."

344. What is Canadian about Israeli Apartheid Week?

The first Israeli Apartheid Week (IAW) was held a the University of Toronto, January 31 to February 4, 2005. Organized by the University of Toronto Arab Students' Collective, it featured lectures, films, demonstrations, and other events to protest Israel's occupation of Palestinian lands. It depicts Israel's actions in terms of the long-discredited policy of "apartheid" associated with the Union of South Africa, and it equates Zionism with racism. Critics accuse IAW of being not only anti-Israel but also anti-Jewish, anti-Semitic, pro-Muslim, and pro-Islam. Since 2005 the annual week of protest has spread to other countries, so that by April of 2009, similar demonstrations were held on campuses in some forty cities, including thirteen in Canada. According to the IAW website, the week of protests is now "one of the most important global events in the Palestine Solidarity calendar." It promotes what it calls BDS (Boycott, Divestment, Sanctions) against Israel and Israelis.

345. What is the Comfort Maple?

The so-called Comfort Maple is a maple tree that is thought to be older than any other maple tree in Canada. It is estimated to be over five hundred years old. It stands eighty feet tall with a trunk twenty feet in circumference and a crown that spreads some eighty feet. It bears the name of the Comfort family of United Empire Loyalists who owned the land on which it stands, now part of the Comfort Maple Conservation Area in the vicinity of the Ontario town of Pelham in the Niagara Peninsula. The tree's scientific name is Acer saccharum. Pelham's official coat of arms shows the tree in red and white, traditional Canadian colours.

346. Who is the Canadian in the partnership of Harman Kardon?

Harman Kardon is a respected name in audio speakers and tuners. The original Harman Kardon company was founded in 1953 in Woodbury, New York, to design and manufacture high-quality home and car audio equipment, first high fidelity and monaural, then stereo components. Sidney Harman and Bernard Kardon were the company's original founders. The latter partner retired from the enterprise in the 1970s, but the former became one of the giants of the American consumer electronics industry. JBL, Infinity, and AKG are their related brand names.

There is no known Canadian connection with Kardon, but Sidney Harman was born in Montreal (there is conflicting information about the year, but possibly in 1917); he was educated in the United States, where he earned a doctorate in public administration. He now heads the top-500 company Harman International Industries, Inc., established in 1980 in Washington, D.C. He has held U.S. government positions and assisted many arts institutions and educational bodies. In September 2007 he was in the news for the opening of the Sidney Harman Hall of the Harman Center for the Arts in Washington, D.C., designed by Jack Diamond, the Toronto architect.

347. What did Eaton's contribute to the Christmas spirit?

The T. Eaton Co. Limited, the now-defunct chain of family department stores, contributed mightily to the spirit of Christmas in Canada.

It introduced Eaton's Santa Claus Parade, which continues to wend its way through the downtown streets of Toronto to the delight of children, their parents, and their grandparents. Santa, in his sleigh, and other festive floats would reach their destination — the main Eaton's store at the intersection of Queen Street and Yonge Street, Toronto. The well-lit display windows of the department store featured animated displays of Santa and his little helpers at the North Pole. Eaton's sponsored the parade from 1905 to 1981. Thereupon, it continued with other sponsors as the Toronto Santa Claus Parade. It is held in mid-November each year and is described as the largest and longest such parade in the world.

Eaton's department stores in the country's major cities introduced their immensely popular Toyland, with magicians, each Christmas season. For youngsters in smaller cities, towns, and villages, there was the Christmas Wish Catalogue, which featured special toys.

Eaton's also introduced the character known as Punkinhead, The Sad Little Bear, for Christmas 1948. With his woolly tuft of hair, he was Santa's mascot and rode behind him in the reindeer-drawn sleigh. Eaton's "answer" to Rudolf the Red Nosed Reindeer, he had his own colouring book and his image appeared on assorted children's merchandise. Punkinhead was created and drawn by Charles Thorston, the Winnipeg artist who worked with Disney, MGM, Fleischer, Terrytoons, Screen Gems, and others, creating or at least recreating a number of animated cartoon figures. Some of these included Snow White (he based her features off his Scandinavian girlfriend), Bugs Bunny (he re-coloured the white hare gray), and Elmer the Safety Elephant (modelled on Disney's Dumbo). The Punkinhead verses and storylines were composed by Beth Pringle Hudson, a member of Eaton's advertising department.

So, Eaton's dynasty of merchants and philanthropists made many and mighty contributions to the spirit of Christmas in Canada. I owe much of this information to Roy MacGregor's imaginative column "Christmas Past," the *Globe and Mail*, December 24, 2007.

348. What is *The Screech Owls* series all about?

The Screech Owls is the general title of a series of short novels about members of a team of peewee hockey players. It was written by newspaperman and novelist Roy MacGregor, and it was published by McClelland and Stewart. The players live in the fictional town of Tamarack, Ontario, and their mysteries and adventures, both on and off the ice, are told by Travis Lindsay, the team captain of the Screech Owls. *Mystery at Lake Placid* is the first title in the series. That volume appeared in 2000, and since then more than twenty-two titles have been published.

What are they about? "Terrorists, murderers, kidnappers, ghosts, and other improbable anomalies befall the preteens in between, and sometimes during, their hockey games and tournaments." Over one million copies of these books have been sold. Exciting stuff and very Canadian!

349. Who invented the game of basketball?

Nobody better described the invention of the game of basketball than Garrison Keillor, host of radio's *The Prairie Home Companion*, for "A Writer's Diary," on January 20, 2010:

> It was on this day in 1892 that the first official basketball game was played, in Springfield, Massachusetts. Basketball was the brainchild of James Naismith, a Canadian who was teaching at a YMCA training school in Springfield, which prepared young men to go out and be instructors in branches of the YMCA. Naismith was teaching physical education, but the winters were cold in Massachusetts, and his students were frustrated that they couldn't go outside. He wanted something physically challenging but that could be played indoors, in a relatively small space. He tried all kinds of new and old games, but nothing

worked. Finally he remembered a game he had played as a kid in Canada, a game called 'Duck on a Rock.' He took a few rules from that and adapted it into a game he called Basket Ball. He nailed peach baskets to the balcony on each side of the gym, but the baskets had solid bottoms, so if anyone managed to get the ball in the basket someone else had to climb up and get the ball down. The rules evolved, and basketball caught on fast, helped by the spread of YMCAs. Naismith helped establish the sport at the college level, becoming head coach at the University of Kansas. By the time he died in 1939, basketball was an official Olympic event.

350. Have Canadians contributed to the Globe Theatre in London?

There are interesting connections between this country and both the original Globe Theatre and the modern Globe Theatre.

Yes, there are three Globe Theatres to consider. The first Globe Theatre flourished during the reign of Queen Elizabeth I. The second Globe Theatre was built following the fire that destroyed the original structure in 1613. The third Globe Theatre, the architectural reconstruction of the original playhouse, was built and is being operated during the reign of Queen Elizabeth II.

Scholars refer to the first and second theatres as the Shakespearean Globe (1599–1642), and to the third theatre as Shakespeare's Globe (opened officially by Queen Elizabeth II in 1997). The shape of all three playhouses is the same: a doughnut-like coliseum with a thrust stage. The first two playhouses seated 3,000 people. The current playhouse, the reconstruction, seats 1,500. As well, the location is the same — on the bank of the Thames River in London, almost next door to the Tate Modern.

According to existing records, the Lord Chamberlain's Men of the first Globe staged productions of fifty-four different plays written by a number of contemporary playwrights. Twenty of these plays were the work of William Shakespeare. The revived company is committed to productions of the Bard's works but is not limited to them.

The reconstruction of the original Globe is credited to the Chicago-born man-of-theatre Sam Wanamaker (1919–1993), who made the project his life's goal. In this undertaking he was ably assisted by John Orrell (1934–2003), who was English-born, University of Toronto-educated, and an Edmonton-based professor of English at the University of Alberta. Orrell's specialty was theatre history and it informs his scholarly work *The Quest for Shakespeare's Globe* (1983). Over many years, Orrell undertook extensive research to establish the dimensions and characteristic architectural features of the original structure, which had been levelled by the Puritans in 1644. Orrell's investigations and scholarship guided Wanamaker and advised the architectural firm that handled the reconstruction. For his pioneering contribution to Shakespeare's Globe, Orrell was posthumously awarded the Sam Wanamaker Award in 2004.

In 1985 the Shakespeare Globe Centre of Canada was established by Christina and Lyle Blair in Toronto to further the causes of the playhouse. As well, the SGCC has offered the annual Christopher Plummer Fellowship Award to permit select Canadian actors to participate in a one month international residency program in London at the Globe. This program is currently in hiatus and SGCC has formed a partnership with Soulpepper Theatre in Toronto. Christopher Plummer and Albert Schultz are patrons.

Independently, David R. Galloway and Donald F. Rowan, both professors of English at the University of New Brunswick, donated their substantial collections of books and research materials, catalogued at the University of Toronto, to the Globe's research department in 1999. It is known as "The Canadian Library."

The design of the original Shakespearean Globe, after a lapse of four centuries, profoundly affected the design of twentieth-century playhouses and their theatrical productions. This came about when British director Tyrone Guthrie bravely rebuilt the Globe's thrust stage (in place of the standard proscenium arch stage) under the makeshift tent at the Stratford Shakespeare Festival in Stratford, Ontario. That was in the summer of 1953, and since then the innovation — actually the revival of the Elizabethan practice — caught on, first in playhouses in Canada and then in those throughout the United States and Great Britain.

351. Is it called the "Stratford Festival"?

The Stratford Shakespearean Festival of Canada was founded in 1952, as a summer theatre, to produce the dramatic works of William Shakespeare and other classical playwrights in the Ontario city of Stratford, a ninety-minute drive from Toronto. In its early years it was advertised as the "Stratford Shakespearean Festival."

In the 1970s and 1980s it was renamed the "Stratford Festival" in an attempt to broaden and extend its appeal beyond the works of Shakespeare. In November 2007, its new artistic director, Antonio Cimolino, announced the decision to re-emphasize the centrality of the Bard by rebranding the repertory theatre the "Stratford Shakespeare Festival."

Whatever its popular name, it currently mounts more than one dozen new productions in its four venues for seven months of each year. These productions include classical dramas, contemporary plays, and musical comedies, not to mention dramatic readings, lectures, seminars, films, and tours.

352. What is the "hockey stick controversy"?

The so-called hockey-stick controversy has nothing to do with hockey or with violence on the ice; it has to do with a graph that illustrates climate change over the past millennium. The graph takes the form of a hockey stick that rests on its edge, its handle at the left with its blade at the right, rising steeply. It represents a thousand years of stable temperatures, followed by an abrupt rise in global warming in recent years. The pattern was observed in those graphs that illustrated estimates of mean temperature changes over the last millennium in North America. First use of the hockey-stick image was made in 2003 and has been attributed to climatologist Jerry Mahlman, head of the U.S. National Oceanic and Atmospheric Administration's Geophysical Fluid Dynamic Laboratory. The image of the hockey stick is a vivid one but it has not saved the statistics behind it from criticism, so the controversy continues.

353. What are some instances of "unparliamentary" language?

Here is an unofficial list of a handful of the words and phrases that have been deemed unsuitable for use in the provincial and the federal parliaments of Canada. A member who uses such language or persists in doing so may be ushered out of a legislative chamber. These expressions date back to the early days of the Parliament of Canada, the Legislative Assembly of Alberta, and the Legislative Assembly of Quebec. Here are some of the expressions, along with the years in which they were first found to be offensive:

Parliamentary pugilist (1875)

a bag of wind (1878)

inspired by forty-rod whiskey (1881)

coming into the world by accident (1886)

blatherskite (1890)

the political sewer pipe from Carleton County (1917)

lacking in intelligence (1934)

a dim-witted saboteur (1956)

liar (consistently from 1959 to the present)

a trained seal (1961)

evil genius (1962)

Canadian Mussolini (1964)

pompous ass (1967)

fuddle duddle (1971)

pig (1977)

jerk (1980)

sleaze bag (1984)

racist (1986)

scuzzball (1988)

weathervane (2007).

354. Does the federal government subsidize federal political parties?

The surprising answer to this question is that the federal government subsidizes federal political parties, and it does so by receipting to those parties $1.95 for each vote they receive in a federal election. In the year 2009, there were roughly 20 million eligible voters, of whom 14 million bothered to cast their ballots.

This practice was instituted by the administration of Jean Chrétien. It was designed to monetarily assist the leading parties following the imposition of a ban on donations from corporations and organizations and a cap on individual donations of $2,200 annually, $3,300 during election years.

According to one survey, these are the sums received by each of the major parties for the election year 2008: Conservative Party of Canada,

$10.5 million; Liberal Party of Canada, $8.7 million; NDP, $5.1 million; Bloc Québécois, $3.0 million; Green Party, $1.3 million. (Fringe parties do not qualify, should they fail to field a sufficient number of candidates or receive a minimum number of votes.)

The Conservative administration of Stephen Harper (despite his party being the major recipient of the federal largesse) tried to eliminate the subsidies in 2009, but there was much opposition from the other parties, especially from the BQ, which relies almost exclusively on the "handout." The proposal to eliminate the annual, per-vote subsidy has met with the approval of many editorialists across the country who see the present program in negative terms: as non-conservative in nature, as an addition to the national debt, and as a "reward" to voters who cast their ballots for any federal political party that runs candidates in only one province and is mandated to seek Quebec's separation from the rest of Canada.

355. What is L'Arche?

L'Arche, French for "the archway," is the name chosen by Canadian-born, spiritual leader Jean Vanier, son of Governor General George Vanier, for the community that he established in the town of Trosly-Breuil, near Compiènne in northwestern France, to care for people with intellectual disabilities. Abled and disabled people live and work together, sharing the same living quarters in a true Christian community.

L'Arche has became an international movement with over one hundred communities around the world. North America's first community was established in 1969 in Richmond Hill, Ontario, by Anne and Stephen Newroth, who had worked with Jean Vanier at the original L'Arche. The Canadian community is known as "L'Arche Daybreak." For many years its pastor was Henri J.M. Nouwen, the Dutch-born priest and theologian who wrote about spiritual subjects and the need to share insights. He died at Daybreak in 1996 and is the subject of the biography *The Wounded Prophet* (1999), written by Michael Ford. Named in his honour is the Henri J. M. Nouwen Catholic Elementary School in Richmond Hill.

"In a world that often sees people with intellectual disabilities as less than whole, L'Arche celebrates their creativity, transparency and great capacity for joy as important gifts to be shared." These words come from L'Arche Daybreak's website. "Life in L'Arche is simple: we welcome four or five people with disabilities to live with four or five assistants. Together we create homes of welcome and celebration, sharing the daily tasks of cooking, cleaning, and shopping: and the assistants help marginalized people to claim dignity, self-confidence, and respect in the home and in meaningful work opportunities. The great discovery for assistants has been that our lives in community have been good not only for them but also for us." So wrote Sue Mosteller, a member of the community.

To mark the fortieth anniversary of L'Arche Daybreak, Jean Vanier videotaped a message of greeting from France: "The objective of L'Arche communities is to be schools of relationship. Many schools exist which help people develop their intellectual capacities. There are many schools of formation for people to develop their abilities and deepen their religious faith. But there are not many 'schools of the heart,' 'schools of compassion,' 'schools of relationship' which help people open up to those who are different and to understand them."

356. What is or was "The Canadian Conspiracy"?

Conspiracy theorists, take note! *The Canadian Conspiracy* is the title of a tongue-in-cheek "mockumentary" that "reveals for the first time" how the Canadian government is subverting the United States by taking over its media. Produced in 1985 by HBO/CBC and directed by Robert Boyd, it stars such Canadian-born American celebrities and luminaries as Lorne Greene, the leader of the "conspiracy"; Lorne Michaels, the protege, who shares the leader's first name; Leslie Nielsen, the government's liaison with his brother Erik Nielsen; Eugene Levy, "the insider who risks his life to bring the conspiracy to light"; John Candy, the lurker; newsmen Peter Jennings and Morley Safer; actor William Shatner; and comic Martin Short. They are hounded by American News Network (ANN) reporters who pester them about the conspiracy, all knowledge of which they deny. Much is made of Leslie Nielsen's brother Erik, then the actual deputy prime Minister of Canada, and of the green card being named after Lorne Greene. It is a clever program about the Canadian penetration of the media — Broadway as well as Hollywood.

357. What is the meaning of the word *chimo*?

An all-purpose Canadian world, *chimo* was derived from Inuit and Indian usage on the West Coast in the late nineteenth century and was later popularized during the Centennial Celebrations of 1967. The Native word has numerous uses. For instance, *chimo!* may mean "hello," "goodbye," or "cheers!" *Chimo!*

Index

Also by John Robert Colombo

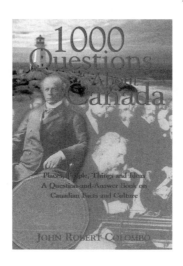

1000 Questions About Canada
A Question-and-Answer Book on Canadian Facts and Culture
978-0888822321
$22.99 £11.99

What are "snow worms"?
Are there more moose than people in the Yukon?
Where will you find the world's largest perogy?
What was Pierre Elliott Trudeau's favourite snack food?
Which province was the last to shift traffic from the left-hand side of
the road to the right?

These are some of the questions that are asked — and answered — in
1000 Questions About Canada. Every reader with an ounce (or a gram)
of curiosity will find these intriguing questions and thoughtful answers
fascinating to read and ponder. This book is for people who love curious
lore and who want to know more about the country in which they live.

The Midnight Hour
Canadian Accounts of Eerie Experiences
978-1550024968
$19.99 £11.99

The Midnight Hour is amazing, amusing, and frightening. It will make you pause to wonder — about ghosts and spirits, fate and destiny, strange beasts and even stranger human beings. The accounts within describe encounters in Canada with monsters and mysteries from 1784 to the present. Editor and anthologist John Robert Colombo derived these true tales from nineteenth-century newspapers, personal correspondence, emails, interviews, and more. The collection is certain to entertain you ... especially during "the midnight hour"!

Available at your favourite bookseller.